SPIRITUAL KNOWLEDGE

Spiritual Knowledge

WATCHMAN NEE

Christian Fellowship Publishers, Inc.
New York

Available from the Publishers at:

Box 58
Hollis, New York 11423

PRINTED IN U.S.A.

CONTENTS

Part ONE: **THE PATHWAY TO THE KNOWLEDGE OF GOD**

1 Dealing by God and Dealing with God   9
2 Knowing God in Prayer and in His Will   29

Part TWO: **SELF-KNOWLEDGE AND THE LIGHT OF GOD**

1 The Way to Self-Knowledge   47
2 The Source of Light   65

Part THREE: **THE RENEWING OF THE MIND**

1 The Nous   85
2 The Renewing of the Nous   95
3 The Nous and the Spirit   105
4 The Way of Renewing   115

Translator's Note

"My people are destroyed for lack of knowledge" (Hosea 4.6). So mourned the prophet Hosea. The glory of the gospel of Jesus Christ is that "all shall know [God], from the least to the greatest of them" (Heb. 8.11). Spiritual knowledge is open to all God's children today. It is therefore not only our duty but also our privilege to seek this knowledge.

In the present volume, brother Watchman Nee attempts to help us to develop this spiritual knowledge. He points out the difference between mental knowledge and spiritual knowledge, shows the ways to the true knowledge of God as well as of ourselves, and explains the relationship between spiritual knowledge and the renewed mind.

Though the messages in this volume were given by our brother in the earlier days of his ministry, the truths contained are nonetheless timeless. They are as applicable now as they were then. These messages were originally published in Chinese in three different booklets, but in view of the interrelationship among them, they are now being printed in English in one volume. May all the children of God "be filled with the knowledge of his will in all spiritual wisdom and understanding, to walk worthily of the Lord unto all pleasing, bearing fruit in every good work, and increasing in the knowledge of God" (Col. 1.9,10).

Scripture quotations are from the American Standard Version of the Bible (1901), unless otherwise indicated.

PART ONE

THE PATHWAY TO THE KNOWLEDGE OF GOD

1 | Dealing by God and Dealing with God

But Jesus answered and said unto them, Ye do err, not knowing the scriptures, nor the power of God. (Matt. 22.29)

And he was parted from them about a stone's cast; and he kneeled down and prayed, saying, Father, if thou be willing, remove this cup from me: nevertheless not my will, but thine, be done. And there appeared unto him an angel from heaven, strengthening him. And being in an agony he prayed more earnestly; and his sweat became as it were great drops of blood falling down upon the ground. And when he rose up from prayer, he came unto the disciples, and found them sleeping from sorrow. (Luke 22.41–45)

Again a second time he went away, and prayed, saying, My Father, if this cannot pass away, except I drink it, thy will be done . . . And he left them again, and went away, and prayed a third time, saying again the same words. (Matt. 26.42,44)

And by reason of the exceeding greatness of the revelation, that I should not be exalted overmuch, there was given to me a thorn in the flesh, a messenger of Satan to buffet me, that I should not be exalted overmuch. Concerning this thing I besought the Lord thrice, that it might depart from me. And he hath said unto me, My grace is sufficient for thee: for my power is made perfect in weakness. Most gladly therefore will I rather glory in my weaknesses, that the power of Christ may rest upon me. (2 Cor. 12.7–9)

For this cause we also, since the day we heard it, do not cease to pray and make request for you that ye may be filled with the knowledge of his will in all spiritual wisdom and understanding, to walk worthily of the Lord unto all pleasing, bearing fruit in every good work, and increasing in the knowledge of God; strengthened with all power, according to the might of his glory, unto all patience and longsuffering with joy; giving thanks unto the Father, who made us meet to be partakers of the inheritance of the saints in light. (Col. 1.9–12)

He made known his ways unto Moses, his doings unto the children of Israel. (Ps. 103.7)

And gathering together all of the chief priests and scribes of the people, he inquired of them where the Christ should be born. And they said unto him, In Bethlehem of Judea: for thus it is written through the prophet, And thou Bethlehem, land of Judah, art in no wise least among the princes of Judah: for out of thee shall come forth a governor, who shall be shepherd of my people Israel. (Matt. 2.4–6)

But a certain one of them, Caiaphas, being high priest that year, said unto them, Ye know nothing at all, nor do ye take account that it is expedient for you that one man should die for the people, and that the whole nation should perish not. Now this he said not of himself: but being high priest that year, he prophesied that Jesus should die for the nation. (John 11.49–51)

For this is the covenant that I will make with the house of Israel after those days, saith the Lord; I will put my laws into their mind, and on their heart also will I write them: And I will be to them a God, and they shall be to me a people: And they shall not teach every man his fellow-citizen, and every man his brother, saying, Know the Lord: for all shall know me, from the least to the greatest of them. (Heb. 8.10–11)

In the first passage we have quoted we find that a few days before the death of the Lord Jesus some Sadducees questioned Him on the matter of resurrection. They said: "Now there were with us seven brethren: and the first married and deceased, and having no seed left his wife unto his brother; in like manner the second also, and the third, unto the seventh. And after them all, the woman died. In the resurrection therefore whose wife shall she be of the seven? for they all had her." To them the Lord gave a most distinctive answer: "Ye do err, not knowing the scriptures, nor the power of God." I do not intend to explain this complicated story, but will draw from this verse two profound principles which concern our spiritual life. The first is understanding the Scriptures and the second is knowing the power of God. These two principles indicate that a Christian should have two kinds of knowledge: first, the knowledge of the Scriptures, and second, the knowledge of the power of God.

Currently the children of God who really seek after Him are divided into two classes: one class knows the Bible but knows little of God's power; the other does not know much of the Bible yet knows the power of God. Very seldom are Christians well balanced in both points. I shall not speak on the relative importance of these two principles; I intend, rather, to say to all that it is not enough just to know the Bible but that we must also know the power of God. Allow me to view you all as those who understand the Scriptures, that I may draw your attention to this matter of the way we know God. Knowledge of the Scriptures alone is not sufficient; we must know God himself. But to know Him requires dealings with God and dealings by God. We will not come to the knowledge of God if we do not deal with Him and expect to be dealt with by Him. For the pathway to the knowledge of God is through such dealings. There is no other way. This each one of us needs to take to heart.

Knowledge of Bible Alone Not Equivalent to Knowledge of God

We recall that one day some people arrived at Jerusalem and inquired everywhere: "Where is he that is born King of the Jews?" They inquired of others as they went around. Herod heard of it and was troubled. He called in the chief priests and the scribes of the people to inquire of them where the Christ was to be born. When the priests and the scribes heard this question, did any of them answer that he must go home and search the Scriptures or that he had forgotten to bring his Bible? No, they instead very quickly recited by memory the prophet and replied: "In Bethlehem of Judea." This reveals how good their Scripture knowledge was. They could give instant answer when asked. Was their reply wrong? Not at all. Yet this was the surprising thing: that after they had answered, none of the scribes or elders started to journey towards Bethlehem. What they knew was most accurate, nevertheless they only told the magi from the East to go to Bethlehem. They were like the traffic policeman who directs people to where they wish to travel though he himself stays put at his post. Although their knowledge was excellent, they themselves did not go and seek the Messiah. These magi might have learned from the writings of Daniel that there would be one born to be the King of the Jews; and hence they traveled a great distance to find the Lord. Is it not strange that those who had little knowledge of the Scriptures sought earnestly the King of the Jews, whereas those having great knowledge of the Scriptures sought Him not? Having traveled a long way to seek the Lord, the people from the East finally found Him. Hence those who have only scriptural knowledge may not know God.

It proves to be true not only concerning the birth of Christ but the death of Christ as well. Was it not Caiaphas who predicted: "It is expedient for you that one man should die for the people, and that the whole nation perish not" (John 11.50)? Yet who condemned the Lord Jesus to death? Who but Caiaphas and his father-in-law Annas? Hence we see how useless it is to have scriptural knowledge without also knowing God. Through the prophecies of Jeremiah God spoke again and again: "I will put my law in their inward parts, and in their heart will I write it . . . And they shall teach no more every man his neighbor, and every man his brother, saying, Know Jehovah; for they shall all know me, from the least of them unto the greatest of them" (Jer. 31.33,34). It is not enough to have merely the outward knowledge of the Bible; such knowledge must also be written upon man's heart. Having it written in the heart results in knowing God. We wish brothers and sisters to realize how inadequate mere mental knowledge of the Bible is. We must seek to know God also.

A lamentable condition prevails today, which is, that few are those who truly know God. Brethren, we may frequently listen to Bible knowledge and yet we still do not know God. He who only possesses some knowledge of the Bible is like one who fights with a mere reed as weapon: he will bend as the wind blows; he has not the strength to fight. Let me ask, Who can say today that he knows God's purpose, God's mind, His will, and His way? I often say that to know God is precious beyond measure; nothing can be compared with it. Some people can open the Bible and speak quite well on a passage, but they may not know God at all. They may talk well, yet they are strangers to Him. The knowledge of the Bible ought to lead us to the knowledge of God. This is not so nowadays.

How to Know God

In the garden of Gethsemane the Lord Jesus prayed to know the will of God. Gethsemane means oil-press. The Lord knew he had to press out the oil there. He knelt and prayed, "Father, if thou be willing, remove this cup from me: nevertheless not my will, but thine, be done" (Luke 22.42). The Bible tells us that He prayed the second time and the third time in the same fashion. He did not pray just once and let the matter drop casually. No, He prayed thrice. And when He rose from prayer, that is, after He finished praying, the Lord came to His disciples and said to them, "Sleep on now, and take your rest: behold, the hour is at hand, and the Son of man is betrayed into the hands of sinners" (Matt. 26.45). When He prayed in Gethsemane He said, "If it be possible, let this cup pass away from me" (Matt. 26.39); but when Peter drew his sword and cut off the ear of the high priest's slave, the Lord declared, "The cup which the Father hath given me, shall I not drink it?" (John 18.11) So during the time of prayer in the garden of Gethsemane the cup seemed to be yet doubtful; but after He arose from prayer He had no doubt about the cup which He was ready to drink. By praying three times He was able to know God. He would not take anything for granted, but would seek to know Him through dealing with God in prayer. There in the garden He dealt with God, as well as He himself was dealt with by God.

There was a thorn in Paul's flesh. I will not try to identify that thorn. Suffice it to say that it was something which made him uncomfortable and which pierced him like a thorn. He also referred to it as a messenger of Satan; so that it must have been quite upsetting. Without the power of Christ Paul would not be able to bear this thorn. He prayed three times, asking the Lord to remove the thorn. But the Lord told him, "My grace is sufficient for thee, for my power is made perfect in weakness" (2 Cor. 12.9). He was now clear on this issue. Did he pray the fourth time? No. For by the third instance the Lord had spoken and the issue was settled by His word. Paul did not decide anything according to his own knowledge; rather, he dealt with God in prayer so as to ascertain what was His will concerning this particular matter.

From the experiences of our Lord and the apostle we discover one principle: if anyone wishes to know God he must learn to have transactions with Him. In other words, he needs to deal with God and to be dealt with by God. Many Christians carelessly let difficulties or problems pass by without receiving dealings from God. They do not know why He sends them these difficulties. These people may read the Bible daily and seem to possess some knowledge and light, yet they are ignorant of the mind of God. Their knowledge is clearly insufficient. For this cause, beloved, we must deal with God and receive dealings from God; and then shall we truly know Him.

In Practice

Let me give an example. We each have some particular sin which easily entangles us. Some are troubled by this sin, while others are caused to fall by that sin. Some cannot overcome pride, some cannot overcome jealousy, some cannot overcome ill-temper, some cannot overcome the world, and some cannot overcome the lusts of the flesh. Each has his special sin. He is aware of it, and he is not able to overcome it. One day he reads in Romans 6.14 that "sin shall not have dominion over you" and in Romans 8.1–2 that "there is therefore now no condemnation to them that are in Christ Jesus. For the law of the Spirit of life in Christ Jesus made us free from the law of sin and of death." He is now in possession of the knowledge of these Scriptures; still he cannot overcome his sin. The truth which he has cannot be put into practice. I am afraid there are many brothers and sisters among us who are in a similar dilemma. If another believer who cannot overcome sin comes to ask him for help, he may be able to speak at large on the great doctrine of how to overcome sin, though as a matter of fact he himself is yet bound by sin. Consequently, the brother who comes for help will return home armed with some knowledge of overcoming sin without the experience of overcoming it. This means that what different ones hear is mere knowledge of the Scriptures; they have not been dealt with by God, and hence know not the power of God.

How, then, do we know God through His dealings? Suppose you are easily irritated. You go to God in prayer about this matter. At the same time you ask someone for advice as to how you may overcome this sin. The brother may tell you: you should ask God to eradicate the root of this sin of ill-temper just as you might do in pulling out a bad tooth. (We wish that this *could* happen, though we know it is absolutely impossible. Sin will not be pulled out, but will anchor firmer the more one pulls! Such advice will not help a bit, since it is totally irrelevant to experience.) After you are so advised, you accordingly pray to God. Instead of having the sin uprooted, you find that it goes deeper in you. Yet you are one who fears God. You will not overlook the sin which you cannot conquer. You must have dealings with God. You will come to Him with prayer—not once, but twice or thrice, asking Him what is the matter after all. In doing so, God will show you the truth of Romans 6.6 that He does not deal with the body of sin but deals with the old man. He does not pull out the root of sin from the flesh but crucifies the old man on the cross.

After a while, you find yourself again in bad temper. So you seek out another brother for help. He may perhaps tell you that since our old man was crucified with Christ when He died, you now need to reckon yourself as already dead, then you shall overcome. You now have gained one more bit of new knowledge.

When temptation comes, you reckon yourself dead. Who would have thought that however much you reckon, your temper still gets out of control. This method is of no avail. Although the Bible clearly states that in reckoning you can overcome, you do not overcome. If you are God-fearing, you will seek the Lord once again. Then you will be shown that your reckoning does not begin with the time of temptation, but more than nineteen hundred years ago you had already died with Christ. Your heart should therefore rest on the finished work of Christ. Whenever temptation comes, you know your old man had died more than nineteen hundred years ago. Consequently you have no need to grasp any word, but simply to rest in what God has already done for you.

Not too long afterwards, however, you again lose your temper when tempted. If you are not God-fearing, you will by this time probably give up. But you fear God, therefore you cannot be satisfied with mere knowledge of the Bible. You will inquire of God again, saying, "O God, Your word declares that my old man was crucified with Christ; why then is it that I still cannot overcome my sin?" You once again parley with God. He may show you wherein you have failed. He may tell you that He has allowed you to fall because you do not know the corruption of your flesh. You depend too much on yourself. Thus you learn another lesson. Knowing yourself—that is, knowing the corruption of your flesh—weans you from trusting your flesh and causes you to beseech God humbly to preserve you.

Nevertheless, as time passes, you once more fall. Being a man who fears God, you will again come to Him and consult with Him, saying, "Why can I still not overcome my sin? I have reckoned my old man as dead, I have known my flesh; why is it that I am yet subject to fall?" You pray once, twice, three times, maybe even a fourth or a fifth time. You plead to God to speak to you. Finally, He gives you revelation. You are made to understand that sin is but a fruit of the tree. Just as the tree of life bears a different kind of fruit each month, so the root of sin produces a thousand kinds of fruit. The root is one, but the fruit multiplies day by day. You are always dealing with one particular sin, yet you neglect other sins. While other sins grow, you return to that old particular habit of sin. In dealing with bad temper, you overlook other sins. And as the manifestations of other sins increase in you, the sin of ill-temper soon follows suit. You forget to deal with your pride and jealousy, your unclean thoughts, your many other sins. If you deal only with your bad temper, the more you deal with it the more you will be defeated. But if you deal with all sins, God will bless you.

Upon obtaining all this knowledge you may assume that you are now traveling on the highway of victory and can therefore spend the rest of your life in peace. Unexpectedly, however, sin reappears and so you fall again. This time it is really critical. You cannot let it pass by. You will approach God once more and ask Him to deal with you. After you have prayed once and twice, you are given a new revelation: How about your life after you have entered into victory? God here shows you that the finished work of Christ can only be maintained in fellowship with Him. He points out to you how your prayer and your reading of the Bible have fallen short, how you get up too late each day, and hence something is wrong with your daily communion with Him. God does not suggest that the work of Christ on the cross has fallen short; He only means to say by this that what Christ has accomplished on the cross must be kept alive in the atmosphere of your fellowship with God himself.

After a few more days, perhaps, you once more lose control of your temper. Again you pray and ask God to deal with you. This time He may indicate to you that everything with you is fine except that you have not kept one special command of His. It may be something which He requires especially of you. You are already moved, yet you make excuses and delay your obedience. As a result, He allows you to lose your victory. Because of your disobedience in this other regard, your former sin (ill-temper) reappears. Therefore, my friends, do not think that because you have disobeyed only once here or once there that you can expect victory in overcoming sin. I have frequently mentioned in the past that the secret of victory is trust and obey. Any weakness at *any* point in obedience will undeniably weaken one's faith.

The Man Who Knows God

If you have been dealt with by God and have come to a true knowledge of Him, you will know at what particular juncture another person cannot get through. You are able to help him because you have perhaps received dealings on this very matter for more than fifty times yourself. You do not speak to men about the Bible only; you speak to them of God.

One summer there was a conference led by many famous people. I was told that I should go and listen to one preacher who preached so well in those days. So I went. He spoke at that particular session on how to be filled with the Holy Spirit. The Scripture verses he quoted were most appropriate. His illustrations were superb, and his presentation was very logical. But after he had spoken for only ten minutes I asked myself, Was this the filling of the Holy Spirit? For although he spoke well, even so, from the few amateurish utterances of his, it was recognized at once that he did not know God in this particular matter. He knew nothing of the filling of the Holy Spirit. For this reason the knowledge of the Bible alone does not give us the knowledge of God nor enables us to speak of Him. We must learn to walk the way of the cross. We need to be dealt with by God. The Lord did not disregard the will of God because He was the Son of God. Instead He prayed once, twice and three times to the Father till He could say, "The cup which the

Father hath given me, shall I not drink it?"

The apostle Paul also prayed and prayed, until he was told by the Lord that His grace was sufficient for him. We know how the Corinthian believers misunderstood Paul. The letters to the Corinthians express his sorrow, as the letter to the Philippians declares his joy. Of all the Pauline letters, only these two are full of self-expression. But I love to read Corinthians more than Philippians. The Corinthian believers mistook him completely. They accused him of being subtle and misjudged him on his sickness. He did not insist that God should remove his thorn so as to escape the mocking of the Corinthians. He only said, "Concerning this thing I besought the Lord thrice that it might depart from me. And he hath said to me, 'My grace is sufficient for thee: for my power is made perfect in weakness'." Because God had spoken, he did not force Him to change His mind. Instead Paul declared, "Most gladly therefore will I rather glory in my weaknesses, that the power of Christ may rest upon me."

None will ever know God without having transactions with Him. I once told a few brothers that there is only one way of making progress in the spiritual life and that is, by receiving God's dealing. If you refuse to accept dealings from God you will never make any advance. Should you only want to obtain knowledge of the Bible, you will merely need to study hard and to be assisted by those who have Bible knowledge. But if you really want to know God, you must have personal dealings with Him, for there is no other way.

I treasure the experience of those who truly know God. From their utterances we may judge how well they know Him. A certain sister from the West was truly one who waited for the return of Christ. (Note that many scholars of prophecy do not know how to wait for the Lord's return!) When I was in her presence I knew I could not deceive her, for a few words from her revealed how familiar she was with spiritual things. I remember how on the last day of 1925 I was praying with her. She prayed: "O God, do You really allow the year 1925 to pass away? Must You wait till 1926 to come back? Even on this last day of the year, I still ask You to come today." I knew what she was praying. After several months, I met her on the road. She took my hand and said, "Brother, is it not strange that He has not yet come?" These utterances showed that she was not just a scholar on prophecy but was one who had fellowship with God and who really waited for the Lord. She knew God. She was an expert on the second coming of the Lord.

Once I met another sister. I thought she was a novice in spiritual things. But after conversing with her for a few sentences, I discovered that she was an expert. She was one who was having dealings with God and was being dealt with by God.

Onc day in Peking I met an elderly believer. He did not have much Bible knowledge, nor was he admired for his practical living; yet he really knew God. During our conversation he said, "Christ is responsible for everything." Though his family was quite poor, both he and his wife were happy. He asserted that in spite of many difficult problems in his life, Christ took responsibility for each one of them. So I asked him, "What responsibility do you bear?" "I am responsible for singing hymns," he answered. This was just like King Jehoshaphat going to war, with singers before the army to sing praises to the Lord (see 2 Chron. 20). I inquired of him further by saying, "You have forsaken all for the Lord's sake. Do you have regrets over what you have done?" He replied candidly, "Why, you don't seem to understand; Christ, not I, is responsible for all these." Concerning this matter of Christ being responsible for all things, anyone can see that this believer is well ahead of us and that we have to learn this lesson from him. He is indeed an expert on this particular aspect of spiritual life. What we must have is not mere Bible knowledge, but knowledge which is learned from God. Oh, only those who have been dealt with by God know what is meant by the dealings of God.

Must Have God's Dealings

You must have your environment dealt with as well as your sin dealt with by God. For instance, do you let things which appear in your family come and go as they please? Or if indeed you pray, do you pray for just once and then stop praying because you have not got an answer? How can you expect to know God? This is not Paul's way. He prayed a number of times till the Lord answered him. If you are willing to pray only once, you better not pray at all. You shall pray once, twice and three times; and should you receive no answer, you must pray ten times, or even a hundred times till God speaks to you.

Let us remember that hastiness ought not have any place in faith or prayer. Faith endures time. If God does not give, we can wait until we are a hundred years old. We hope against hope. Abraham believed God (Rom. 4.18). Elisha told King Joash to shoot the arrow upon the ground, but the king did so only three times and stayed his hand. Because of this, the prophet said to the king that he could only smite the Syrians thrice, whereas if he had struck the arrows to the ground five or six times he would have been able to smite Syria till he had consumed it (see 2 Kings 13.14–19). Such too is our prayer, that we cannot pray two or three times but then stop.

A servant of the Lord once said, "Prayer is like placing name cards on a balance. You put a one ounce weight in one side of the balance, and add card after card to the other side. When the first card is thrown into it, it cannot raise up the one ounce weight. Card after card is put in, but the weight is still unaffected. Then perhaps at the very moment you throw in the last card, the weight on the opposite side is at last lifted. So it is with prayer. You pray once, twice, three times, and once more. Maybe this is your last prayer, but then the answer comes."

For this reason, let us learn to have transactions with God. We must ask for God's dealings concerning our mortal bodies, our works, our families, our environments, and all our happenings. I knew a sister who was more than sixty years old. She had claimed that nothing in her life was accidental. I asked her whether her statement was true and she answered positively. I thought she might make such a statement during preaching but it certainly could not be true in fact. Once a brother had a cold, and she wrote to that brother asking him what lesson he had learned through this cold. I imagined it was all right to ask a person who had contracted typhoid fever whether he had received any instruction from God, but how could one ask a person if he were taught of God in the circumstance of a common cold? Nevertheless that brother was really helped by her. He wrote back, saying that he was not at all concerned in the beginning, but having been asked he was awakened, and thus he was dealt with by God and was changed.

There was another brother who had sickness in the family. Again, the sister wrote to tell him that he ought not let this sickness pass carelessly but should take up the responsibility of prayer for the sick in the family. That brother was indeed helped by her.

Once she herself was sick in bed. Her co-worker had departed for another place, her cook had gone home for some reason, and she had no money left. She kept on praying in bed, asking God why she should be ill at this time. God showed her that this sickness was not of Him but was due to the attack of the enemy. So she declared: "If I myself have anything wrong, I can be sick; but if this is a Satanic attack, I ought not be sick." She had already had a high fever for four days, yet she instantly got up. Now it was at this time that this sister composed the following hymn:

> To the foe my word is always 'No',
> To the Father it is 'Yes',
> That His plan and all His counsel

be accomplished with success;
When Thine orders I'm obeying,
   grant me, Lord, authority
To fulfill Thy plan eternal
   through the Spirit's power in me.

And upon finishing this hymn she went out to do work, and her sickness was gone.

Whatever situation she was in, this sister saw the hand of God in it. She knew well what is meant by the victory of Christ. Once she told me, "If only you knew the victory of Christ." I could easily discover from the Bible such passages as Colossians 2.14,15 which tells of the triumph of the cross of Christ, or Hebrews 2.14 which speaks of how through death the Lord Jesus renders powerless him who has the power of death, or 1 John 3.8 which states that the Son of God appeared to destroy the works of the devil, or Revelation 12.11 which proclaims that the brethren overcame Satan because of the blood of the Lamb. Yet each time I heard this sister mention the victory of Christ, the word seemed to convey a special meaning in her life. This was something beyond my comprehension.

Once I suddenly got ill while I was staying in her home. At that time I was not only physically uncomfortable but also mentally disturbed by a few things. She came to see me; so I told her my condition. But each time after I said something, she would look intently at me and say, "Christ is Victor." To which I said, "I do not mind this physical illness but I shiver with cold sweat when the inward burdens are not solved." She came back again with, "Christ is Victor." I replied: "This is not so. You may claim the victory of Christ over Satan, you may claim the cleansing of the precious blood over sin; you may claim healing over sickness because Christ has borne our infirmities. To all these you may say Christ is Victor. But now I am at fault. I have not yet been reconciled with God, so how can you say 'Christ is Victor'?" Neverthe-less, she still insisted that Christ is Victor. She read to me two Scripture verses. There and then I came into the clear, both within and without. On that very day I began to understand the meaning of Christ our victory. Formerly I had only the scriptural knowledge of the victory of Christ, but now I learned a new knowledge from God. I commenced to see that the victory which I had had before was as a weapon made of reed which was totally ineffective. I now realized the all-inclusiveness of the victory of Christ. It includes victories over the enemy, our sin, our sickness, and over all things. Having been repeatedly dealt with by God, this sister knew what the victory of Christ is. And because she knew God, she was able to help others.

Today many believers pay little attention to the Bible. May I ask which of the sixty-six books of the Bible you are most familiar with? How sad that many Christians do not even master one book of the Bible. But sadder still is it that they do not know God in a real way. If we want to know Him we must not let anything pass by negligently, be it something in the family, of the physical body, or in the environment. We should have dealings with God. We need to pray till we get His answer. Through transaction after transaction we learn our lessons till we come to a true knowledge of God.

The Knowledge of God and Work

Let me also say a few words to workers. No one can work for God if he does not know God. Many think that they are qualified to preach after having studied the Bible in theological seminaries. Let me ask this question: In preaching the gospel do we go out to explain the Bible or to proclaim the Savior? To expound the Word or to tell the good news? Even if these seminaries are ideally good, they can only help people to understand the Bible but not to know God. Nowadays there are many who understand the Bible, many who can analyze the Word well, but how many can speak of God and of the way to know Him? Should we desire to work for God, we must first learn to know Him.

Some declare that they like to do the work of personal evangelism, they hope they could preach to others; but when they actually come to people, they have nothing to say. Indeed, what could they talk about? A person can only preach that word which has moved him. He is only able to help people with what he himself has been touched with by God. What can anyone really preach if he does not know God?

Let us illustrate this with an example. There is a certain sin in your life which does not seem forsaken. The hand of God always touches on this point. Whenever you pray, God will speak to you about this sin. He will not let you go until this sin has been dealt with. Then next time when you meet a brother who is in a similar condition, you now realize that Bible knowledge cannot solve his problem, for he must have his sin dealt with. But in case you are careless about your own sin, you will forgive the brother who commits the same sin as yours. In forgiving him you are simply forgiving yourself; you cannot help him.

If a brother has been dealt with and apprehended by God on the matter of early rising, he will lay his hand on another brother who is a late riser and say, "Brother, rise up quickly, for the manna is melting away." Having been dealt with himself by God, he is now able to help other people.

Preaching is to preach that which God has dealt with in your life. Otherwise, however you preach, you will not be able to lead people to that point. There are so many preachings today with so little results, because the preachers themselves have not been taught through the dealings of God. It is better not to open our mouths if all that we preach is but some teaching—the result of two or three hours of preparation on the sermon. We need to have three or five years of experiencing God's dealings before we are fit to preach. If we deal with a few things which happen each day, we will be qualified to deal with people who have the same problems.

Do you know the difference between sermonizing and testifying? Sermonizing cannot help, but testifying does. You may compose a sermon which gets the approval of man, yet you cannot send people successfully on their way, for there is no foothold. It is similar to a pupil in elementary school who tries to write an account of a trip he has never taken. Not so with testimony. As you testify, you are describing the actual situation—as though you are holding out the very thing you are talking about. You may not speak well, but you cannot speak wrong. For you are depicting an actual scene which is both visible and touchable. Therefore, in working among believers and unbelievers alike, a matter of great importance for us is to have transactions before God. Only what we have had dealings about are real; and these will touch people as we speak.

Brothers and sisters, there are tens of thousands of things that require God's touch today. How regrettable that up to the present we have overlooked so many things without ever having received God's dealings. If we learn to accept God's ways with us day by day, we shall know Him after a while. Many believers rush here and there to hear and to ask people, but they do not seek the Lord in themselves. No wonder they still do not know God after having been saved for many years. How pitiful is this condition! We ought to inquire of God what we should do with this or that matter. We should seek till we know God's will. We must not pray just once and stop. I repeat, If you pray only once, it would be better for you to cease praying altogether.

In conclusion, then, let me say that lazy believers can never expect to know God. I would also say to those who serve God that you will not be able to make people feel if you have not been made to feel pained yourselves. May we daily learn to deal with God as well as to be dealt with by God. Such experiences are most precious. It is more valuable to know God than to have mental knowledge of the Bible. May He bless us all.

2 | Knowing God in Prayer and in His Will

For we walk by faith, not by sight. (2 Cor. 5.7)

Concerning this thing I besought the Lord thrice, that it might depart from me. (2 Cor. 12.8)

And he left them again, and went away, and prayed a third time, saying again the same words. (Matt. 26.44)

Let us continue to probe into this matter of how to know God. We need to learn to deal with Him as well as to be dealt with by Him. In others words, learn to have transactions with Him. Earlier we only mentioned how to deal with God, but that alone is not sufficient. Now, we will speak of two further matters, which are (1) how to know God in prayer, and (2) how to know God in His will. If we do not know the nature of God and how to commune with Him, we are not able to go on spiritually.

1. KNOWING GOD IN PRAYER.

One thing which puzzles Christians is how we can obtain God's answer in prayer. Each Christian must have this desire of having God hear his prayer. That believer will be an abnormal Christian if God hears his prayer only once in three or five years or once in three or five months. Many hardly have any experience of God answering their prayer. I do not mean they do not pray. I only mean their prayers are ineffective. Many believers have no assurance that God would hear their prayers. They do not know if He has answered or not until they have gotten what they pray for. They have no conviction whatsoever in the beginning. As Christians we ought to be spiritually rich, but we become poor because we know not how to pray. How poverty-stricken we are if our prayer is heard only once in three or five years! I have mentioned many times that no Christian can live under the state of unanswered prayers. How terribly we must have fallen.

Today I would like to consider with you how a Christian should pray. How soon should his prayer realize an answer? What confidence does he have after prayer? What will be the final issue? Now where can we get all this knowledge? We can get it through knowing God. If you were to put these questions to different people they would probably tick off to you more than ten articles pertaining to prayer, such as the forsaking of sin, that one must have faith, and the necessity of praying according to the will of God. The problem is that many know prayer only through the Bible; they do not know prayer in the presence of God. They read the Word and ferret out the conditions for answered prayer. All these are learned from the Bible, not from dealings with God. They are therefore not of much use. We must spend time before God and learn to deal with Him as well as to be dealt with by Him. Thus shall we gradually come to know what He requires of us in respect to prayer. To know God in prayer does not come by chance, nor by hearing, nor by what I say now. A travel guide can only point out a place to a person, but it does not bring him to that place. If he does not go there, he will not have any experience of that particular place.

Brothers and sisters, suppose you have a wish—a petition within you which you want God to fulfill for you. You will pray to

Him concerning this matter. You may pray fervently or casually, pray at length or briefly. Yet the strangest thing is, you never think of knowing God in such a time of prayer. You do not really mind if God answers or does not answer your prayer. For instance, you ask God to give you a book; and if one day He gives you that book, you take it as a reward from Him. You ought to know, however, that it is not just a book you get. You also obtain a knowledge of God. Indeed, you learn how to pray so as to get an answer from Him. Receiving a book is very insignificant, but knowing how to pray and to be answered in prayer is a most precious piece of knowledge. Through this time of prayer you come to know God a little more. Our knowledge ought not to come from reading the Bible alone; we must have it also directly from God.

Remove Any Hindrance

Let us continue with our example of the book. You ask God to give it to you. You pray for four, maybe five days, with no answer. You pray for two months—but still no answer. You pray for three, perhaps four months; yet the answer is still delayed. You do not understand why God does not give it to you. You need to have a seeking and a searching heart. You ask yourself why it is that God answered last time but does not answer this time. Where lies the fault? You know the fault cannot be on God's side, for He is well able to give. The fault, then, must be on your side. You temporarily lay aside asking for the book and seek to find out the cause of prayer unanswered. You may ask God, "O God, I have asked You to give me a book; why then is it that You withhold it from me?" When you are really seeking for understanding, God will tell you that you need to have this or that thing in your life dealt with. Only after you have had these dealt with will He answer you. So you proceed to remove these hindrances. And after three or five days, God gives that book to you. Hence what you get is not only a book but also an advanced knowledge of God. Such knowledge will make your next prayer different from your former one because you know you must remove whatever needs to be removed before God will answer your prayer.

It is evident that the knowledge you and I obtain from God comes through hard dealings, not merely from hearing or reading. If, in each matter, you have to deal with God as well as to be dealt with by God—that is, learning to have transactions with Him—you will know what He requires of you, what He wishes to remove from you, what it is He desires to accomplish in you. Then shall you know Him.

Desire

There are many spiritual principles in prayer which we ought to learn, or else we will not have our prayers answered. Here is a practical illustration. You may ask God for a watch. You pray for three or five days, and then you forget it. God has not answered your prayer, so you discard it altogether. You often pray like that. You have prayed for hundreds of things in this fashion. God does not answer, and therefore *you* forget and *God* forgets too. Such prayer is equal to no prayer. According to normal procedure you should investigate why God does not grant you a watch. You should inquire of Him. And as you deal with Him in this instance He will cause you to know one thing, which is, that your desire is not strong enough. Since your desire is not at all strong you will not feel touched if God in fact answers your prayer nor will you, on the other hand, sense loss if He does not answer you. Under such circumstance He cannot answer your prayer. A prayer which does not move the pray-er's heart cannot move God's heart. For this reason, one must have a perfect desire before God; which means that you will not let the matter go if God does not answer you. How can you expect Him to answer if you can so easily drop the matter regardless if your prayer is answered or goes unanswered? Here you learn a new bit of knowledge, that there must be real desire in all your prayers.

Ask

There is yet another side. Sometimes your heart is full of desire, but you still do not have it. As you go to inquire of God you will be shown that you indeed have a desire yet you have not asked, you have not opened your mouth and uttered your desire. This is precisely what the Scriptures say: "Ye have not, because ye ask not" (James 4.2). And so you receive another new piece of knowledge: there needs to be an asking outside to correspond with the desiring inside.

Obedience

Do you really want God to answer your prayer? You may have asked without and desired within; nevertheless your prayer still goes unanswered. You consequently pray and pray, inquiring of God why He does not answer you. He may indicate that you have not listened to Him in a certain matter; hence He will not hear you. You need to hearken to Him before He will listen to your prayer. In this way you learn that you must obey God. And when you have obeyed, you can pray: "O God, I have removed what You wished me to remove. Now, answer my prayer." You thus come to further new knowledge—that God only listens to the prayer of those who obey Him. How far apart is the knowledge which you learn through God's dealings and dealings with God from the knowledge which you learn through hearing or reading the Bible.

May I speak candidly? Many brothers and sisters fail to have God hear their prayers because they have not learned obedience. If we do not listen to God's word, He is not able to answer our prayer. We let many things go unnoticed, considering them as very minor; but God does not permit them to pass by. Many Christians need to be strictly dealt with by God. How can we get on if we let things go unattended? Without dealing with each and every item carefully we will not be heard in our prayer. In time of great peril God may hear us as an exception. But if we seek to have Him always hear our prayer we must obey Him in every respect.

Faith

Perhaps you have obeyed. Your prayer, however, still goes unanswered. The watch does not make its appearance. You go to God and inquire of Him once more. He may tell you you are lacking in faith. You seek to find out how you can have faith. Again and again you approach Him requesting that He answer your prayer and grant you faith. Yet you do not get what you ask. Possibly He will show you that unless certain things are first dealt with you will not have faith. Or He may indicate to you that you are too anxious in your prayer and that your anxiety reveals your unyieldedness. Unless you yield, and say, "O God, I will submit even if You do not give it to me", your prayer will not be answered. This appears to be contradictory to what was said earlier about the heart's desire. Indeed, many spiritual things do seem to be contradictory; nonetheless they are all facts. Yet at this juncture God says you may now ask for faith. You therefore ask; and one day, when you come to a passage in the Bible, certain words there lay hold of you. It is not you who lay hold of the word, but the word lays hold of you. The words seem to loom larger than usual before you. You instantly recognize that this is the consolation which comes from God. This is the word God gives to you. You realize then and there that He has already answered your prayer and has given His promise to you. Based on the word which He has granted you, you speak to Him and have transactions with Him. In this way you obtain new knowledge, a knowing how to believe God in prayer. You begin to understand what is meant by faith mentioned in the Bible.

Praise

Everything has been dealt with, and there is also faith, yet the watch does not arrive. You pray on for another month or two. The more you pray, the less sure you become. Hence you inquire of Him. By this is it made known to you that you should praise and not pray after having received the promise. If you pray after having received the promise, you will pray in doubt. Since God has already given you a word and you are in addition in possession of faith, you ought instead to praise. Satan will come to tempt you and suggest that you should pray; but you will answer, "No, I must praise." He will tempt you again, saying you ought to pray; you will nevertheless insist, "No, God has already answered my prayer; so I will praise." You do well if you praise. Even in human relationships, you will certainly ask if there is no promise; but once the promise is given, you give thanks. Since God has promised you, you ought to praise Him. But if you continue to pray, you will pray away your faith.

Someone who has had deep experience with the Lord will warn us not to pray away our faith. For what we may do is to pray out faith and pray in doubt. To pray on shows that we do not believe what God has already told us. Here we learn from God still another form of new knowledge: knowing how to praise after having received faith in prayer.

Reminding God

After repeated praises, the watch is still not in hand. You inquire of God again as to the reason. You may learn that having come into faith and praise, you must also remind God. Just as God says through Isaiah, "Put me in remembrance" (43.26). It is as if God could forget and He needs you to stir up His memory. He has already promised; now He wants you to remind Him. Be it clearly understood that you are not to remind God with a heart of unbelief, rather, you say this to God with faith. "Do remember what You have promised." This is what Solomon did when he prayed: "Now therefore, O Jehovah, the God of Israel, keep with thy servant David my father that which thou hast promised him" (1 Kings 8.25). Such reminding is very meaningful. Due to delay, you are given opportunity to deal with God and so learn something new about Him.

Deeper Lessons

Even after you have done all these, you may still sometimes fail to obtain what you pray for. For there are more lessons to be learned. In this matter of prayer, we may think it is so simple that even a child of six or seven years old can do it, but it is equally so profound that after seventy or eighty years there is still much to learn, much remaining unknown. Perhaps God wants you to wait, perhaps you need to learn how to resist the assault of Satan. It is through all prayer and petition that you learn to know the ways of God. And the next time in prayer you know how much you ought to have removed. You are able to get to the promise of God. Advanced believers are quite confident in their prayers. They know God will hear without any shadow of doubt. If you do not know that He will hear you, you will be full of doubts and become restless. Therefore, learn to know God in all things—both big and small. Practice this, and He will soon hear your prayer.

Some Experience

I had a friend who once was in need of one hundred and fifty dollars (if I remember correctly). At that time we lived in a village, and it was already Saturday. He needed that money for the following Monday. The ferry ran only a few times during the week and no ferryboat operated on Saturday and Sunday. He had only two dollars in his pocket. So, he prayed to God. God showed him that he still had two dollars and today was only Saturday. He should wait till next Monday. He obeyed God and wished to know how he should spend the two dollars. Going out to preach the gospel, he met a person who told him that he had not yet collected the wage for cleaning his windows. Whereupon he paid the man a dollar. My friend now had only one dollar left in his pocket. He went on, and met a beggar asking for alms. He first thought he should change the dollar into dimes and then give half to the beggar. This one dollar suddenly became quite precious to him. Yet on second thought he knew this was wrong. So he gave the whole dollar to the beggar. As this dollar went out, God came in. He was exceedingly happy, for, he said, I now have nothing in the world to depend on and therefore God will take care of me. He returned home and slept peacefully. On the Lord's Day he served as usual. The following Monday a friend wired him one hundred and fifty dollars, the remittance charge of which alone ran as high as thirty to fifty dollars! He was able to cover his need without any lack.

Each time we expect God to answer our prayer we must learn to receive His dealings. Not a drop of the ocean can enter into the bottle if it is sealed with a small cork. The two dollars in our

pocket are like the small cork; unless it is pulled out we cannot receive anything from God. Although we can learn a great deal at
once, our experience should deepen as the years go on.

As you keep on learning, you will discover that even the words
used in prayer are related to prayer answered or not answered.
You know what to utter in order to *get* an answer, and you know
what can be uttered for a prayer *not* to be answered. You have
searched every aspect of prayer. Learn to pray with confidence.
Do not wait for three or five months before assurance is given. No
one has the experience of knowing God without knowing Him in
prayer.

A sister in the Lord, Miss Margaret E. Barber, once felt that
God wanted her to prepare ten odd rooms in the form of a hostel
in order to receive believers. She prayed about this matter.
Strangely enough God caused an industrial school to nearly cease
operation. Consequently, the school was rented to her. It had
twenty rooms, and the rent for each month was twenty dollars.
The thing was thus settled to my great surprise.

But something more surprising happened later. Four years had
passed and bad news came that this industrial school was to be reopened. I learned of this from my father, for he was one of the di-
rectors of the school. So one afternoon I paid a special visit to this
sister. I asked her if she had heard the news. She told me that she
had already been informed by the authority that the school would
be reopened in the fall and that they had also engaged two engineers from the United States who were already on the way. According to their knowledge the school was definitely to be opened.
I asked her whether she was thinking of moving. Her answer was
no. I asked further if she had prayed. She said no, for there was no
need to pray. A young believer standing nearby voiced the opinion
that she must be deceived by Satan this time. She answered,
"Wait and see." I asked her how she could have such confidence.
She told me that God would never play with her. If God wanted

her to have a hostel, who could drive her out except God ordered her to stop? For He never makes fun of us. But, the engineers had already started on their journey and the school was planned to be reopened!

She quietly went to the mountain for her summer vacation as though nothing had happened. A surprise came just before she came down from the mountain. The school authority suddenly sent her a letter informing her that the school would not be opened and asking her to continue renting the building. What had happened was that in the course of the preparation for opening the school a great catastrophe occurred, and for certain reasons the finances of the school were liquidated! Oh, if only we learn accurately the way of God, we will know how to meet any situation which may arise, thus avoiding many unnecessary actions and unneedful words. If we know God we know how He will act towards a certain matter, just as we can predict the word and action of a person if we know his temperament. Should we know God, we can ascertain whether or not He will answer certain prayers.

Nowadays the church lays much stress on Bible study. True, Bible study is important. But I have been beseeching you all that it is even more important to know God. If you learn these lessons you will know exactly how to help people who are groping in darkness. Though the case may be different, the principle is the same. As you pray with a person, you know whether his prayer will be answered. As you pray with two people, you know whose prayer will be answered and whose will be unanswered. This does not mean that you have become a prophet. It simply indicates that judging by their spiritual condition you are able to learn the results of their prayers.

Let us never be satisfied with our prayers going answered or unanswered. How precious it will be if each prayer receives its sure answer.

2. KNOWING GOD IN HIS WILL.

If we wish to know God's will, we need to have dealings with Him. Those who have no such dealings know not God's will. Some brothers and sisters may think it impossible to know such a tremendous thing as the will of God. True, God is most sublime. Will He tell us most insignificant people His will? It is important to prepare ourselves. If a mirror is unclear, the picture it reflects will be blurred. Or if it is unevenly ground, it will even distort the figure it reproduces. Should we be unready, who can tell how much we may misunderstand God! Each time we wish to know His will we must first deal with ourselves. We need to lay ourselves aside, willing to forsake everything; then He will reveal His will to us. Each time we seek God's will we must have ourselves dealt with by Him.

When George Muller sought to know God's will, he examined himself time after time. In his diary he often began his first entry touching upon a given matter with such words as, this or that thing seemed to be so. At the second entry, he wrote again that it seemed to be so. Later on he might record that after two month's examination this same matter still seemed to be so. On a certain day certain people came with a request which appeared to be related to this matter. On still another day a co-worker said something to the same effect. On yet another day, though, there came a promise. After many days, he recorded something like, Now this matter was clear. Still later, he wrote that it became clearer, for there was not only word but even also supply. Finally, he entered in his diary that it was now perfectly clear. Sometimes he revealed in his diary that although the money in hand was not much, God had begun to supply and bless. He was not afraid of being laughed at, nor did he sign any contract with men. Whenever there was need, he asked God to supply that need, and He never failed him. He always learned how to deal with God.

Once in his prayer he felt that God wanted him to visit Germany. He told Him there were three obstacles to his going: one, if his wife went with him, who would take care of their three children; two, there was no traveling money; and three, he would need a person to manage the orphanage for him. He acknowledged that he did not know if it was God's will for him to go; but if it was, he asked God to make provision in these three respects. Afterwards, a man came to him one day who was most suitable to take care of the orphanage. So he told God that one obstacle was removed, how about the other two? Later on, a mother moved to his home for a few months. She could take care of his children. The second obstacle was overcome. Still later, someone sent him a personal gift (for he never used the money designated for the work), which solved his third problem. Because of all this, he inquired of God if he could now commence his journey. Entries like the above were clearly recorded in his diary. He learned to deal with God step by step.

The Story of Abigail

Mr. Muller once taught a little girl how to pray. Her name was Abigail. For a long while she was thinking of getting a multicolored woolen ball for a toy. She was very young. One day she saw the man of God come to her home. So she consulted with him, saying that, having heard from her parents that he knew well how to pray, she would ask if he was willing to pray for her that she might get a multi-colored woolen ball.

The elderly Mr. Muller answered that he would pray for her but that she must also pray. The child knelt down and this man of God knelt down by her. The girl prayed first, saying that she wanted a woolen ball in multi-color. Afterwards, this man of God bowed his grey-haired head, putting his hand on her and prayed:

Here is a child who wishes to have a woolen ball in many colors. Nobody knows about this, and I too will not do anything about it. This is Your business. Please hear her prayer. Upon ending these words, he waited for a few seconds as though he was still saying something to God. Then he got up and told the child that in two days God would give her the woolen ball to play. Her little heart leaped for joy. This elderly man had brought her to God. She thought in her mind: perhaps her grandmother would bring her the colored woolen ball or maybe her aunt would do so.

To her surprise, on the second night who but her own father brought her the ball! She was overjoyed. Her father had a department store. He had sold every ball except a multi-colored woolen one. This ball had been on display too long to be any longer presentable. So he took it home and gave it to the little daughter to play with.

The next day Mr. Muller saw her, and he asked whether she found the colored woolen ball most interesting. He did not ask if she had gotten the ball; rather, he asked whether she found it interesting to play with. This man who knew God had confidence.

There were many such little incidents in Muller's life. Of course, he had learned this after several decades. But learn he did. He had followed God for over ninety years, and his many experiences were learned from Him. He was never careless about anything. He always recorded in his diary how this or that thing was today. He was clear on everything. He was having dealings all the time. It is no wonder, then, that he had such deep experiences. The error with people today lies in their mistaking the knowledge of the Bible to be spiritual knowledge, not knowing that true spiritual knowledge is learned from God. If anyone desires to learn before God, he has to deal with Him as well as to be dealt with by Him.

Dealings and Knowledge Are Inseparable

The most precious thing in our life on earth is to know God. In order to know Him we must receive His dealing in all things. We must receive His dealing in the matter of knowing His will as well as in the matter of prayer. We need to deal with environment as well as with sin. We shall ask for the meaning of everything which comes our way. Is there any demand of God? The slothful can never know Him. We know Him through prayer; we know Him through fellowship with Him. We ought to learn from Paul, how he prayed to the Lord not just once but twice and three times until the Lord spoke to him. We should also learn from our Lord, who in the garden of Gethsemane prayed: "My Father, if it be possible, let this cup pass from me; nevertheless not as I will, but as Thou wilt." He prayed not once, but the second and the third time until He was clear in this matter. Let us also pray a first, a second, and a third time till we get God's answer. Only in this way can we know God.

May I say a few words to my co-workers? You cannot go out to work if you have not learned how to deal with God as well as how to be dealt with by God. For you cannot be compared even with a good Christian. If you neither know God's way nor His procedure nor His nature, then what makes you different from other people? You can give them some spiritual ideas, but you cannot lead them on in the spiritual path. Not all who read the guide to Hanchow or Peking have been to Hanchow or Peking. Not all who have a cook book have tested all the food in the cook book. Likewise, you cannot guide people if you have nothing but the knowledge of the Bible.

Yet it is not sufficient, either, to have only experience without the knowledge of the Word; for then one will not have adequate words with which to help people. The Lord says: "Ye do err, not knowing the scriptures, nor the power of God" (Matt. 22.29). Such is His reproach. Many believers are lacking either in knowledge or in knowing the power of God. Many have only a little spiritual idea; each imagines things without really knowing what they are. Some are able to teach other people because their brains are stronger and they can remember a little more of the doctrine. Oh, brothers and sisters, this is too tragic a phenomenon. May we learn to know Him both in His will and in prayer. We are able to know Him. Nothing is more important than this. Let us not store up the light which we have in our brains, rather seek to know God and to receive His dealings.

PART TWO

SELF-KNOWLEDGE AND THE LIGHT OF GOD

1 | The Way to Self-Knowledge

I believe God would have me deliver today a message on how we know ourselves. There has never been a Christian who ever made progress in the spiritual life without his knowing himself. Then, too, a Christian cannot progress spiritually beyond what he knows. According to the light (and not just the knowledge) he receives, so his life shall be. No one is able to advance further than the light which God has given him. The person who neither realizes his fault nor knows his real condition will ever seek for the new or press forward.

One essential part of the Christian's spiritual life is to judge himself, reckoning his flesh as undependable and useless; for only then will he wholly trust in God by walking in the Spirit and not in the flesh. It may be said that without this self-judgment spiritual life is impossible. If we do not know ourselves, how can we judge ourselves, and wherein will we receive spiritual blessing? Not perceiving the corruption of the flesh as God would like us to see, we are totally unable to live a pure life in the Holy Spirit. Due to the lack of self-knowledge, we will unconsciously be filled with self-confidence, and so fail to comprehend what the Lord has said, that "apart from me ye can do nothing" (John 15.5). Although the Holy Spirit is given to help our infirmity, we fail to look for His help since we do not see our weakness. Consequently, we remain in weakness.

Furthermore, not knowing ourselves, we will be so self-conceited as to deem ourselves superior. With the result that we will be filled with pride—that thing which is most abominable in the sight of God. Due to the same lack, we shall also have many deficiencies in our daily life: a number of duties will go unfulfilled, we will engage in some unrighteous transactions with people, an absence of love will emerge in certain areas, and there will be frequent manifestations of impulsiveness, anxiety, and enmity. Yet we are not aware of these things, and hence complacency can set in and further deterioration can result. It is impossible to estimate how much spiritual blessing we have lost since we do not comprehend how perfect and precious is the salvation of the Lord.

Self-knowledge is, then, the first condition for progress. For only those who know themselves would aspire for more excellent things, even God's best. Those who do not know themselves would not be filled with the Holy Spirit since in their hearts they are neither hungry nor thirsty. We conclude, therefore, that self-knowledge is absolutely imperative.

Does Self-Knowledge Come from Introspection?

By what means do the people of this world come to know their own faults? They use the method of introspection. They try to examine their own conduct by recalling the past. They actually "turn within themselves" to scrutinize their heart intent and outward behavior. Introspection is what people commonly call examining one's own heart. Without this exercise they have no way of knowing themselves.

Now I often hear Christians say: "I am going to examine myself to see if anything is wrong," but let me tell you that *introspection is not a Christian obligation.* It is instead a great deception; it has damaged many a Christian. In order to show that introspection is not a Christian obligation, we will ask the following questions: (1) Is there a charge or command regarding introspection to be found in the Bible? (2) Does introspection really yield self-knowledge? and (3) Is introspection profitable?

1. Is there a charge for introspection in the Bible? Is it true that the Bible never charges a Christian to examine himself? Griffith Thomas once noted that there are only two passages in the whole Bible where self-examination is mentioned, but that each one of them has its special scope. Let us now look at these two passages.

"But let a man prove [or *examine,* AV] himself, and so let him eat of the bread, and drink of the cup" (1 Cor. 11.28). The "examine" here does not refer to a Christian examining himself in the pursuit of holiness. It points particularly to the examination of ourselves with respect to our recognizing the bread and the cup as the body and the blood of the Lord as we come before Him to eat the bread and drink the cup. Since our eating the bread and drinking the cup is a testimony, we ought to examine ourselves as to whether we remember the real spiritual significance, lest it become a mere ritual. Hence the introspection here is directed towards asking ourselves if we come to the table of the Lord to remember Him. It does not call us to turn within ourselves to scan our faults so that we may make spiritual progress.

"Try [or *examine,* AV] your own selves, whether ye are in the faith; prove your own selves" (2 Cor. 13.5). Once again the call to examine our inner condition is related to a particular sphere. In Corinth many people at that time spoke evilly of Paul, even questioning his apostleship. Paul therefore asked them to examine themselves if they were in the faith. For if they were, then this in itself constituted the evidence of Paul's apostleship. If God had not called him to be an apostle to the Gentiles, how could they in Corinth have been saved? Since God had called him to preach the gospel to the Corinthians, they were saved; and such salvation proved that Paul was a true apostle. Suppose they were not in the faith; then he would be a false apostle. Therefore, the introspection here is not related to self-examination in the pursuit of holiness, rather is it a special act related to a special situation. It is to prove if there is faith.

Now recognizing that both of these passages relate only to the examination of particular matters, we dare to conclude that the Bible does not charge Christians to be introspective.

2. Does introspection give self-knowledge? So far as our experiences go, we have to confess that introspection does not give us self-knowledge. We will search the Scriptures instead, and see what *they* tell of us.

"The heart is deceitful above all things, and it is exceedingly corrupt: who can know it?" (Jer. 17.9) Our heart being such, how can introspection be trustworthy? For we will be examining ourselves with a deceitful heart; and it is inevitable that we will be deceived by this deceitful heart. For instance, we may be wrong, yet the heart will instead justify us. Or, we may not be wrong but only weak, yet the heart will condemn us as being wrong. Were the heart perfect, it could serve as a standard. Since it is so deceitful, however, how can it be the rule? To use such an inaccurate standard to measure ourselves must without doubt lead to deception.

Once, a person wished to install a pipe on his oven. He measured the length with his ruler and asked the coppersmith to make a ten-foot long pipe. When the pipe was delivered, it seemed to be a foot too long. It would not fit. He reprimanded the coppersmith for the mistake. The coppersmith measured it again with his own ruler and found it was exactly ten feet. But the customer insisted that it was a foot too long. Finally, the coppersmith examined the customer's own ruler and discovered that it was sawed off a foot.

This was done by the customer's child as he was playing with this ruler. No wonder, then, that the measurement always ended up a foot longer. Our hearts are like that sawed-off ruler, an untrustworthy standard.

If we really want to examine ourselves, let us first ask whether we are trustworthy. Our self is so corrupted that God deems it to be no good; how then can we employ *it* for the purpose of introspection? Many people consider this inner exercise a virtue, but may I differ by saying that it is a great error.

We should realize how very complicated is our inner constitution. Our will, thought, and emotion—together with the working of the heart—are highly intricate. It is impossible for us to analyze them thoroughly and understand their inter-relationships. Given such a complex situation, our introspection can never give us an accurate self-knowledge. For when we examine our own feeling we do not know how much it is affected by, and involved with, other things. Consequently, the knowledge which comes from our own feeling is undependable. A slight influence may alter our feeling completely. Frequently we fail to make a right judgment on a certain matter or lack an accurate knowledge of our motive because there is in us some hidden sin, some wrong thought, some little prejudice, some natural inclination or countless other small hinderances. The very complexity and instability of our beings cause us to be inaccurate in our judgments.

As a result, we often encounter such paradoxes as the following. A person may be quite strong on a certain point, yet not only is he unaware of it, he even feels weak in that regard. On the other hand, he may be very weak on another point, yet he is totally unconscious of it and thinks himself strong notwithstanding. These are common occurrences, and they clearly tell us one thing: that in spite of introspection there is no real self-knowledge.

I had a friend, who upon being saved spoke frequently of Christian love. He considered himself full of love. Who knew that he was not at all reconciled to his wife at home? Do you think his self-examination was trustworthy? If one's self is undependable, his introspection is altogether useless.

"Who can discern his errors?" asks the psalmist (Ps. 19.12). No one can. By our own selves we cannot accurately know our faults.

3. Is introspection profitable? Not only does the Bible not contain any command for introspection, but in addition our experience tells us how impossible introspection is. As far as spiritual life is concerned, introspection is very harmful. It may produce either one of two consequences: If the fruit of such an experience is not self-contentment, it will be despair: self-contentment, because of reckoning oneself as being quite good after self-examination; despair, because of finding himself full of flaws. There will be no third consequence.

"Looking unto Jesus" (Heb. 12.2). In the original there is something more in the word which lies between "looking" and "Jesus." It should read "Looking *away* to Jesus" (Nestle's *Interlinear Greek-English New Testament*, also *The Amplified New Testament*). The idea is, that before you can look to Jesus you must first look away from what you should not look at. Our spiritual life is based on looking to Jesus, not on looking into ourselves. If we disobey the command of the Scriptures and look into ourselves instead of looking away to Jesus, our spiritual life will incur tremendous damage.

I have spoken before that self-analysis, which is analyzing one's own feeling, intention and thought, is most harmful. Griffith Thomas once said it was a maxim current in his day that if you wished to look at yourself once, then you should look at Christ ten times. May I alter it by saying that you should look at Christ ten times but look not even once at yourself.

Two years ago I read a fable about a centipede and a frog. During their conversation the frog asked the centipede, "You have so many feet, how do you walk? When you walk, which of your hundred feet moves first?" So the centipede tried to figure out which foot moved first. No matter how he tried he could not put forth one foot. He became so disgusted that he declared, "I do not care, I am going." Yet before he could make a move, he was again thinking of which foot moved first. He was thus completely paralyzed. After a while the sunlight broke through the cloud. When he saw the light his heart was so enthralled with it that he just ran after the sunlight. Gone was his concern over the order of his foot movement. He was actually moving forward. Now this fable can serve as a mirror to our Christian life. Whenever we turn to look at ourselves we are immobilized and cannot advance; but if we look at the light of God, we shall unconsciously move ahead.

Several years ago I read in the *Overcomer* magazine an article entitled "What is Self?" The writer stipulated that self is nothing but recalling ourselves and dwelling upon ourselves. This word is truly profound and is also very practical. Whenever we think of ourselves we become active in ourselves, for we know that the soul is self-conscious. After the Welsh Revival of 1904–1905, a professor visited Evan Roberts the revivalist. They were together for a whole day and talked about many things. Later on he wrote an article telling of his impression of Mr. Roberts. He concluded that Evan Roberts was a man totally unconscious of himself. Our failure lies in thinking of ourselves too much. We remember either our virtues or our defeats, both of which hinder Christ from being fully manifested in our lives.

The way to victory lies not in analyzing ourselves incessantly, but in looking off to Jesus; not in recalling the evil thought but in remembering the good thought; not in getting rid of what is ours, but in letting Christ so fill us that we forget all that is ours. The moment we recall ourselves, we cease to move ahead. The Bible does not exhort us to reflect on how we are, it calls us instead to run by looking away to Jesus. If we turn to examine ourselves we will find ourselves lost in the mist; if we look to Jesus, we will doubtlessly run well.

When I first learned to ride a bicycle I often rode into walls and bruised my hands daily. I accordingly asked a schoolmate who knew how to ride a bicycle to instruct me. For my habit had been that as I rode, my eyes were always fixed on the handles of the bicycle. I had assumed that if my hands were steadier I would be able to ride the bicycle straighter. What puzzled me was that the more I looked at the handles because I wished to steady my hands, the more my hands would shake and the more askew would the bicycle run. My schoolmate told me where my fault lay—I had been looking at the handles of the bicycle instead of looking off at the road. This explained why the ride was crooked and why the bicycle was always bumping into the walls. If I wished to ride straight without hitting any walls my eyes should always look at the road ahead. Is it not true as well with our lives? By turning to look at ourselves we will undoubtedly be defeated. We should always look ahead.

The failure of many Christians can be attributed to introspection. Even if there is no other damage, self-examination will at the least retard the progress. Many Christians have the habit of reviewing the day's affairs after a day is over. Such introspection is self-deceiving. Paul disregards criticism; he will not even judge himself. "Wherefore judge nothing before the time, until the Lord come, who will both bring to light the hidden things of darkness and make manifest the counsels of the hearts; and then shall each man have his praise from God" (1 Cor. 4.5).

Paul knows that only when the light of the Lord shines is one able to discern what is right and what is wrong. If a Christian considers himself over and over again he is sure to be defeated. As he thinks upon his virtue, he will grow proud and will esteem himself more excellent than his contemporaries. And when he sees his fault, he will become downcast and depressed beyond measure. But the knowledge of self which comes by God's enlightenment will not produce such adverse effects.

The Right Way

Now by all this that we have just said we do not mean to suggest that we may live casually, neither inquiring into the right or wrong of our conduct nor probing into the pureness or impureness of our motive. Our understanding is simply that the Bible has not called us to be introspective, though it certainly does not object to self-knowledge. Recalling ourselves is harmful, but the relaxing of ourselves is even more harmful. God never allows us to be licentious. Though He does not want us to indulge in self-examination, He does want us to know ourselves. For when the Holy Spirit is come, He will convict the world in respect of sin (see John 16.8). What the Bible teaches is that we should not seek holiness through introspection; yet the teaching of the Bible will not dissuade us from pursuing after holiness. The Word is opposed to the idea of attaining self-knowledge through introspection, but it *is* for self-knowledge.

Man's error is in considering self-examination and self-knowledge as inseparable; man therefore concludes that rejecting self-examination means rejecting self-knowledge. He does not know that self-knowledge is necessary, only it should not come by introspection. The objective is right, but the method has to be changed.

Since the Bible does not advocate introspection, how can we have self-knowledge? Let us read two passages from the Psalms: "Examine me, O Jehovah, and prove me; try my heart and my mind" (26.2). "Search me, O God, and know my heart: Try me, and know my thoughts; and see if there be any wicked way in me . . . ." (139.23,24) These two passages show us the right way to self-knowledge. If we desire to know our heart and mind, to know our thoughts whether there is any wicked way, we should not spend time in examining ourselves as to how we feel about our own selves; rather should we ask God to examine and search and try us that we may have an accurate knowledge of ourselves. Our self-knowledge comes not by our self-examination but by God examining us.

These passages tell us that if we need knowledge about ourselves *we must ask God to inform us of this knowledge.* This is the most accurate knowledge, for God knows us better than we know ourselves, because all things are naked and laid open before Him. Even the secret recesses of our heart that are beyond our analysis and sensation are not hidden from Him. If we are granted His eyesight we will not be deceived but shall know our real condition.

God's knowledge of us alone is beyond any mistake. Do you know how God thinks of you? You consider yourself to be pretty good; but do you believe God thinks of you that way too? Or you may regard yourself to be quite bad; do you think God agrees with you? Hence do not reckon yourself good or bad according as you feel. Such knowledge is most inaccurate. Only God can tell whether you are really good or bad.

God does not want us to be introspective; yet not because He denies us self-knowledge or allows us to live carelessly, but because He realizes we will never know ourselves through introspection. What He judges as wrong we may consider as good; what He condemns as unclean we may deem as a negligible fault. He is pleased with our having the same viewpoint as His. He will therefore not have us follow our own undependable feeling and inaccurate judgment but He would have us get the mind of the Spirit that we may have His judgment as our judgment.

God's Light and Self-Knowledge

By what means do we know how God looks at us? How can we enter into God's thought concerning ourselves? Psalm 36 contains the answer. "In thy light shall we see light" (verse 9). The word "light" is mentioned twice in this verse and means something different each time. The first light is special, being "thy light," which is God's light. The second light is general, hence no qualifying word is placed before it. God's light represents God's knowledge, His view, and what He sees. "In God's light" points to something being revealed by God, our being told of what He knows of us. The second light shows us the actual condition of a thing. Hence the meaning of this verse is: Having received God's revelation and being enlightened by His holy light, we are enabled to know the exact situation of a matter, for it appears in our eyes as clear as light. In our own light we will never be able to see light. Only in His light shall we see light.

Ephesians 5.13 tells us the use of light most distinctly: "All things when they are reproved are made manifest by the light; for everything that is made manifest is light." The use of light is to manifest. Hence the first light mentioned in Psalm 36.9 is objective in nature, for it is God's light. As we are in that light, we are made manifest by it, causing us to see our true condition. This is seeing light in the light of God. Formerly we did not know our condition; now, with the enlightening of God's light, we see it. Many things which we deemed excellent in the past appear awful to us now when the light of God shines on them. We may consider ourselves as better than anybody else; but one day, when God's light shines, not only our evil looks evil, even our good seems to be evil. It is not a telling the Lord after we have examined ourselves; it is instead a confessing to the Lord upon our being enlightened by God's light.

For this reason, introspection is not a virtue but a huge mistake. The way to know ourselves is not by introspection but by God's light. In His light we may obtain knowledge to know ourselves. As God's light concerning us is exceedingly bright, so in His light shall we see everything as He sees it.

Now you have no need to inquire as to when God's light comes, nor do you need to ask how you can be sure it is God's light. It is not needful to light a candle or kindle a light in order to know the sun in heaven. If you see yourself you know you are under the sunlight, because the sun has already risen. In like manner, whenever you are clearly able to know yourself—seeing your true condition and realizing the corruption of your flesh—you know you are already in God's light because He has given you His light. On the other hand, if you do not view yourself as seriously as the Bible has described, nor believe that your flesh is weak, wicked and corrupted as the Scriptures have defined, it is indicative of the fact that you have not received God's light and that you are not walking in His light. It is not necessary to ask where light is or what light is. As long as you see the effect of light, you know the what and the where of light.

After Adam ate the fruit of the tree of the knowledge of good and evil, the first thing he was aware of was his own shame—he was naked. This was the *feeling of his own conscience*. He felt ashamed; yet did he fear God? No, he still pursued his own way. He made for himself an apron of fig leaves with which to cover up his shame. Later on, when the voice of God was heard to say "Where art thou?", Adam hid himself from the presence of God among the trees of the garden. He now had no way out: he could no longer rely upon the apron he had woven but had to confess that he was naked.

Here we see that the consequence of a man's introspection will at least give him, as it did Adam, a seeing of his own shamefulness;

nevertheless the man will not feel sorry for his sin but will try instead to cover it up. Yet after he was questioned by God, Adam really knew himself. God asked him, "Where art thou?" Did not God know where Adam was? He certainly did. He so asked, however, in order to enable Adam himself to know where he was. All who are experienced believers can testify that under self-examination people may see some fault of theirs but will try to cover it over by their own way. But whenever anyone is enlightened by God's light there is no way left for that one to hide any more.

Once a lady asked a Jew whether he wished to be saved. He answered no. But that lady persuaded him to kneel down with her and to pray, asking God to enable this man to know himself. The light of God came and he began to know how very unclean he was. He saw his own sins; so much so that he wished the ground would open up and swallow him!

This incident shows that unless the light of God shines forth no one can see himself a sinner. Many a person before he is saved is unable to acknowledge himself a sinner. In the eyes of other people he may be a real sinner, yet he himself does not sense it. Only when God's light comes does he know how very sinful he is. The self-reproach produced by the light of God is truly something beyond any self-delusion.

Someone may know he has sinned. He both feels it in his heart and confesses it with his lips. From a human standpoint he would be viewed as having insight of himself. However, when the Holy Spirit brings in God's light upon him that person begins to realize how superficial was his own confession of sin, because he has yet to hate sin as God hates it. Only after he is enlightened will he fully sense the sinfulness of sin and so seek to be delivered. And just here let me address a few words to God's workers. We who work for God should not use our arguments to convince people of their sin; instead, we should ask the Holy Spirit to convict the world of their sinful deeds. *All* kinds of introspection are equally shallow, unfilled, and inaccurate. The light of God alone can cause people to see their real condition as God sees it.

We Christians are able to know ourselves day after day not because of self-analysis but because of God's light. As we are enlightened by His light we immediately recognize the total depravity of ourselves. How often we appear to be quite loving to others, yet once the light of God strikes we will not only see our deficiency in love but also many other defects. Oftentimes we consider our works most successful—we having won many souls—but wait until God's light shines and then we will perceive how empty, unprofitable, and fleshly are these works. We may think we follow God's will with singleness of heart and desire nothing for ourselves, nevertheless when God's light shines we discover how much of God's will has not been kept.

Once I asked a sister in the Lord of her experience in doing God's will. She replied: "Each time God delays telling me His will, I conclude that there must still be in my heart an improper motive or an unwillingness to do His will. This conclusion I have come to as a result of many experiences." Whenever we seek God's will and get no answer, we should ask God to examine us lest there be any unwillingness in us. As God's light shines, we shall behold our inward situation. Do you think there is absolutely no disobedience in you? You have deceived yourself. Whenever we wash our face do we try to detect by introspection if there is white paint or a black stain or any dirt on our face? Do we not use a mirror to reflect back to us whatever may be on our face?

To see ourselves we need to ask God to enlighten us with His light instead of examining our own selves. Frequently we reckon our motive as perfect, but the light of God shows us how selfish, calculating, and unrighteous we are. Without God's light we often consider our lives as passable; in His light, though, we know how unable we are. In God's light shall we indeed see light.

The difference between a deep Christian and a shallow Christian is in the measure of God's light each has—more or less, permanent or temporary. Black is black and white is white under God's light. A shallow Christian may sometimes know his particular fault under God's special and occasional illumination, but a deep Christian is always under God's enlightenment and knows himself.

Some of us may have this experience: when we listen to the testimony of a young believer as to how much he loves the Lord and how he has consecrated all to Him, we sometimes have the feeling that this young man does not know what he is saying. For he has yet to learn how difficult this life of consecration is. He does not realize what awaits him in the future. He is only speaking under the impulse of his current feeling.

Is this not similar to what the Lord Jesus said to James and John? They had requested of the Lord, saying, "Grant unto us that we may sit, one on thy right hand, and one on thy left hand, in thy glory." But Jesus answered with: "Ye know not what ye ask. Are ye able to drink the cup that I drink? Or to be baptized with the baptism that I am baptized with?" And they replied: "We are able" (Mark 10.37–39). They had no idea of how deep and far-reaching the Lord's words to them were, hence they abruptly answered that they were able. Before we have God's light we are like these two disciples. We do not know how weak we are, nor do we realize how much God requires of us. We assume we are capable of anything. But when God's light shines on us, we begin to see how all that we say with respect to many things or to many truths are mere words, because we do not at all comprehend their meanings.

When God's light comes, not only our good shall be made manifest as being no good, even our no good that which we usually acknowledge as such—shall become exceedingly ugly. Oftentimes we are quite aware of our weakness in a certain matter. We ourselves feel it that way, we even tell people about it, and moreover we pray to God concerning it. Nevertheless we lack a deep conviction about this weakness of ours, and are not really convinced of its wickedness. Though we sense a weakness, we are nonetheless able to live on. Only after the light of God has dawned upon us will there be that confirmative view of our weakness and will there grow in us an abhorrence towards it. We cannot live unless we are delivered. The distance between the self-knowledge gained through introspection and that which is gained in God's light is immeasurable.

Therefore, my friends, without the light of God whatever you know about yourself is unreal. Self-knowledge obtained from self-analysis merely represents what you think of yourself; while self-knowledge received through God's light stands for what God thinks of you. Our own judgment can never be as accurate as God's judgment of us.

Here we notice the difference between God's light and knowledge. Knowledge shows what *we* know, that is, what our mind comprehends. God's light is what *He* knows and *is revealed to us by His Spirit.* A great number of people mistake mental knowledge for the light described in the Bible. Consequently we often hear people say, "So-and-so has plenty of light, but his life is not so good." What they do not realize is that light is not knowledge per se. Does not the Bible say, "Knowledge puffeth up" (1 Cor. 8.1)? But when God's light shines into a person's heart, far from it causing him to uplift himself, it will make the person sorry unto repentance—he will hate his flesh and will beg God to deliver him from his uncleanness.

It is possible to be filled with Bible knowledge and at the same time be totally lacking in the light of God. Knowledge discovered in the power of the Holy Spirit is God's light; while God's light stored and memorized in the human mind becomes knowledge. There is no doubt that knowledge as well as experience has its proper place in the Bible, yet knowledge severed from the Holy Spirit's power is dead.

C. I. Scofield once said that nothing was more dangerous than the divorce of truth from power. We may know lots of truth and possess great knowledge, but if these are not in the power of the Holy Spirit we will have no light by which to show us our true condition and to guide our steps. In case we receive light from God we should keep what we have in the Holy Spirit that it may continuously be the light for our path without losing its power.

Many a time God grants us light that we may see the true picture of a thing. At that moment we seem to have seen its innermost depth so as to have the whole thing laid bare before our eyes. After a while, though, we begin to lose the sharpness of its image though we still retain the knowledge of our experience. The light of God has passed off the scene; all that is left is knowledge. (Note: even so, we must at least walk according to our knowledge. However, this does not suggest that knowledge alone is sufficient, because light is very necessary.) Light is able to give us a profound impression which knowledge cannot give.

In order to walk in God's course we must have the light of God. Our own feeling tends to excuse us if it does not totally deceive us. To follow our feeling in the pursuit of holiness can be likened to following a blind guide. Only God's light will make manifest the true state of a matter. Light represents God's view. If God says it is wrong, it is wrong indeed. If He says it is one hundred percent wrong, then it is one hundred percent wrong. Before light comes, you are thinking; it is therefore untrustworthy. The estimate of your life must come from God.

After a dear sister, Miss Margaret E. Barber, passed away, her Bible was willed to me. In one place in her Bible was written the following statement: "O God, grant me a complete and unrestrained revelation of my own self." How profound is this note. Frequently we are unjustifiably satisfied with ourselves because we have seen nothing, not recognizing that God's thought is higher than our thought. Unless we possess His viewpoint we are simply deceiving ourselves. We must dare to be enlightened by God in having our true state revealed to us. Except by the light of God, we have no way to know ourselves. Our own estimate is totally undependable.

2 | The Source of Light

Where Comes the Light?

First of all, Christ is our light. "Again therefore Jesus spake unto them, saying, I am the light of the world: he that followeth me shall not walk in the darkness, but shall have the light of life" (John 8.12). The Lord Jesus is light. As we draw nigh to Him we see light. How often we imagine that nothing is wrong, but when we bring the fact to the Lord and ask Him to reveal the truth to us we realize how very wrong is the matter. Day by day we fancy everything is fine, until we draw nigh to the Lord and then we discover our fault. For the one estimate is our own measurement, while the other is God's measurement. If a Christian does not pray earnestly, asking the Lord to unveil to him his real condition, it is almost certain that nine out of ten times he will do the wrong thing. The more one draws near to the Lord the more shall he receive the light of God.

Second, God's word is the light. "Thy word is a lamp unto my feet, and light unto my path"; "the opening of thy words giveth light" (Ps. 119.105,130). Probably we are quite familiar with these two verses; still, if we meditate on them carefully before God we shall come to appreciate how profound they are. Concerning the path you are taking, is it man or is it God who says you are all right? The work of the flesh cannot be hidden from God's light. Not what people say, but what the word of God says. Right or wrong is not to be daily determined by our feeling, rather is it to be decided by God's word. *We* must not conclude; rather, let God's word judge the matter. Place ourselves before His word and allow it to judge and to unveil. Hence let us study the Bible diligently and depend on the Holy Spirit to open up His word so that we may know ourselves.

Third, Christians are our light. "Ye are the light of the world" (Matt. 5.14). We usually take this word as referring to the good conduct of Christians. Actually it has a deeper meaning. What is said here is that a Christian is a light. He is able to make manifest the true image of a person. As he lives in God's light he is much feared by others, for in seeing him they feel condemned. A feeble Christian does not mind meeting another similar to himself; but when he comes near to one who lives in God's light he feels ashamed. Under enlightenment his pride and dishonesty are all exposed.

Brothers and sisters, no one can work for God without having God's light. Who else will ever be brought closer to God unless "your" light shines on him? If you live close to God and your life is always governed by God's light, you will automatically make manifest the real condition of those who come near to you. To do God's will and to fulfill God's work you need to be a light.

When you draw near to a person who lives close to God you feel His presence. The person does not make you sense how gentle and humble he is; he makes you sense God. When I began to serve the Lord I was determined to do the will of God. Naturally I felt I had done His will. But whenever I went to see a certain sister to talk with her and to read some verses of the Bible together, I was immediately convinced of my inadequacy. Each time I saw her I felt something special: God was there. By getting near to her you sensed God, for she had light, and her life was governed by God's light. As you came near to her, her light would convict you.

One thing, though, must be remembered, which is, that the light you receive is from the revelation of the Holy Spirit, regardless whether its unveiling comes through approaching Christ, studying the Word, or gathering with other believers. It is the Holy Spirit who manifests to you the unapproachable light in which God dwells—even God's glory and holiness and righteousness. It is the Spirit who causes us to realize what is the absolute standard of God by which we are enabled to see ourselves, our real condition, and our shortcomings.

The Power of This Light

The power of this light is to give people self-knowledge. When one enters into this light he is shown his actual condition.

Many a believer is naturally self-conceited, self-complacent, and self-righteous. Human words—exhortation, persuasion, warning and reproach—are unable to help him see his depravity. Only the light of God which shines on him can make him realize how undone, corrupted and hypocritical he is. When God's light comes, everything will betray its true color.

It is true that none can be saved without the shining of God's light on him. But neither can any advance spiritually or work effectively without it. Let us look at these two matters more closely.

How does a sinner come to know that the Lord Jesus is Savior? Without a doubt it is not by argument. Moreover, how does he realize that he is a sinner? No amount of logic, reason, or warning will ever cause a sinner to see his sin and to see the Lord Jesus as his Savior. I do not mean that these are totally useless, for they do have their place. Even so, these can only effect mental consent but not spiritual *seeing*. Every sinner is blind; such blindness prevents him from perceiving the true radiancy of God's gospel. The Holy Spirit, however, opens his eyes that he may see the light of God. Seeing is a special blessing of the New Covenant. That God reveals His Son in me is an experience shared by each and every saved sinner.

How futile for us to think that we may persuade people to accept Christianity, to believe in the Lord Jesus, and to become Christians by beautiful thoughts, reasons, hot atmosphere, emotion, music, tears, and arguments. The chief factor in conversion is God's light, the light which is shed abroad by the Holy Spirit. For the basic need is for a sinner to *see* his own condition as well as to see the glory of the Lord Jesus. Tears, remorse, zeal, and wonderful feeling are all of them of no avail; only seeing in the Holy Spirit can cause him to truly accept the Lord Jesus as Savior. No one is able to believe and accept what he does not see. Because he has seen inwardly he is able to believe. Such faith is immovable and stands up well in trial.

In similar fashion, the growth of a Christian's life does not depend so much on encouragement, warning and teaching—as though these would stir up his zeal to fulfill his duties in praying and reading the Bible. All these are auxiliary, not primary, agencies. The principal factor is in the Christian's *seeing*. For this very reason, the first thing Paul did when writing to the Ephesian believers was to pray for them that God might *enlighten* the eyes of their heart by the Holy Spirit, even though he knew they were quite good in the Lord and were not so morally degraded as the Corinthian believers. The progress in the Christian life is effected by having the light of God, by our eyes being opened to know the riches of God's glory and the exceeding greatness of His power which is given to us through the resurrection of Jesus Christ. How can a believer advance in life if he does not see the abundance of God's grace in Christ Jesus?

All who do special works for God are people enlightened by Him. Only the enlightened know how to judge their own flesh. And those who judge their own flesh are alone used by God. It is when the light of God comes that a believer begins to appreciate how holy God is but how unclean he is. Because he sees the righteousness of God, he realizes his own unrighteousness. By seeing the glory of God, he is convicted of his utter depravity. Having obtained such self-knowledge, he, like the truly circumcised, will depend wholly on God's Spirit and dare not depend at all on himself. Indeed, he will not only distrust himself but will deeply hate himself as well. Such are the workers who are in God's hand and are used by Him. They have the spiritual insight into God's plan and purpose.

Due to the lack of God's light, many a person deems himself superior. Satan often deceives him into imagining he has already attained to sinless perfection. He does so because, not having God's light, he is ignorant of the corruption of his flesh. Now I am one who fully believes that Christ, being our life, will enable us to overcome sin completely. Hence, from my point of view, no Christian can excuse himself by saying that it is impossible for any on earth not to sin. But the possibility of our being victorious over sin does not suggest that our flesh is no longer corrupted.

A common error is to fall into extremes. Some people hold that since we are so corrupted we cannot help but sin; while other people maintain that having accepted Christ as our victory our sinful nature is annihilated in us; therefore we are no longer corrupted. The truth is that in Christ we are victorious, but in ourselves we are corrupted. A believer may live by Christ daily and live a life completely victorious over sin, but at the same time sense daily his own utter depravity. His sense of utter depravity does not inhibit his victory, because it is Christ in him and not himself who is victorious. Neither does his complete victory take away his sense of total depravity, since the corruption of his flesh will not change its nature through the deliverance of Christ.

In order to help those who, having been deceived in their own dim light, deem themselves most holy, sinless, and perfect in love, we will search the Scriptures and learn how many of the excellent and matured saints mentioned there viewed themselves in the light of God.

Job. Job was upright; even God said so. During his trial his three friends agreed that he must have sinned against God. Job himself disagreed, and spent much time arguing with them—trying to prove his purity and righteousness. We all know that later, when God appeared to him, he confessed, saying: "I had heard of thee by the hearing of the ear; but now mine eyes seeth thee: Wherefore I abhor myself, and repent in dust and ashes" (42.5,6). God's light finally came, and so he knew how horrible he really was. Human words could not convict him, but God's light humbled him.

Isaiah. Before God sent forth Isaiah He showed His glory to him. Under this glorious light God's prophet could not but cry out, "Woe is me! for I am undone; because I am a man of unclean lips, and I dwell in the midst of a people of unclean lips: for mine eyes have seen the king, Jehovah of hosts" (6.5). During the time prior to his seeing the vision his lips were already unclean and he had already been dwelling in the midst of a people of unclean lips, yet he was not aware of any of this. He had probably considered himself fit to be a prophet for serving God. But as God's light shone upon him he began to see his actual condition as well as the state of the people around him. How could he be God's mouth if his lips were so unclean? He even cried out, "Woe is me! for I am undone!" God's "holy" will elicits from us our "woe" indeed. Now after Isaiah had received such self-knowledge, a seraph came and cleansed his lips with a live coal. Here we notice an excellent order: first the uncleanness, then God's light, followed by self-knowledge of uncleanness, then the possibility of being cleansed, and finally his being sent out.

Daniel. In the Bible there are only two men whose sins were not recorded. Daniel was one of them. This indicates how much he was favored of God. Even so, the Word tells us that when he saw the Lord and was thus enlightened, "there remained no strength in me [Daniel]; for my comeliness was turned in me into corruption, and I retained no strength. Yet I heard the voice of his words; then was I fallen into a deep sleep on my face, with my face toward the ground" (10.8–9). In God's light even the saint of saints could not stand up, but must fall upon his face toward the ground.

Habakkuk. When Habakkuk was enlightened of God, he had the same experience. Said he, "I heard, and my body trembled, my lips quivered at the voice; rottenness entereth into my bones, and I tremble in my place" (3.16).

Peter. We know how self-sufficient Peter was, yet when he chanced to meet the light of God in the Lord Jesus he could not help but confess his own sinfulness. Recall the story of how the fishermen disciples had toiled all night and had taken nothing. The Lord, though, ordered them to put out into the deep and let down their nets for a draught. As they followed this order they enclosed a great multitude of fishes and filled two boats. Such manifestation of a ray of the glory of the Lord caused Peter to fall down at Jesus' knees, saying, "Depart from me; for I am a sinful man, O Lord" (Luke 5.8).

Paul. This Paul who had fought the good fight, had finished his course, and had kept the faith testified to us shortly before his departure from the world by saying, "I am the chief of sinners" (see 1 Tim. 1.15). Let us notice that the word "am" is in the present tense. This reveals to us his own appraisal of himself. He knew that the Lord Jesus came into the world to save sinners, of whom he was the chief. He had nothing to boast of, having neither merit nor work. Just as the other sinners had been, he too was saved by the grace of Christ. Nay, he considered himself worse than the rest; hence he needed the Lord's grace more than anybody else. Yet who had more of God's light than Paul? But having received more light, Paul knew himself better than others and so judged himself more severely. He who knows not his own self will deem himself holy, advanced, and special. He has had no self-knowledge because he has not obtained the light of God.

John. During the days when our Lord hid His glory in the flesh, this beloved disciple of His was closer to Him than were the rest. We remember he was the disciple who leaned upon the breast of the Lord. Several decades after the Lord's resurrection, and having rendered excellent service, he was especially commissioned by the Lord to write a letter dealing with fellowship, in which he spoke particularly on God's love and God's light. According to man, such a disciple should not be so fearful of the light of God as should many other people. Yet we notice that when the glory of the Lord Jesus was manifested to him on the island of Patmos he saw the Lord's countenance that it "was as the sun shineth in his strength"; and John said, "When I saw him, I fell at his feet as one dead" (Rev. 1.16,17). No one can see God's light without falling to the ground.

Not only from the Bible do we learn of men who humbled themselves, confessed their sins, and knew their own selves through the light of God; we also learn from church history how many of the holiest believers have realized their own weakness and corruption by drawing nigh to God's light. Those Christians whom we will mention in the following paragraphs have generally been recognized as being the most extraordinary believers in the church; yet their own views on themselves are exceedingly abased. This is due to no other reason than the fact that the closer one lives to God the more he knows his own weakness. He who receives more of God's light invariably sees more of his own corruption. The proud and the self-righteous have not seen the light of God.

Martin Luther. When he was in jail, Martin Luther wrote a letter to an influential person in the Roman Catholic Church saying, "You may think that I now am powerless, for the Emperor can easily silence the cry of a poor monk like me. But, you should know that I would yet fulfill the duty which the love of Christ has placed on me. I have not the slightest fear of the power of hades, much less the pope and his cardinals." * Seeing himself in God's light, however, this most courageous reformer could not refrain from crying out: "I dread my own heart more than the pope and all his cardinals. For within me is the greater pope, even self!"

John Knox. For the sake of Christ this Scot had been a teacher, missionary, prisoner, slave, wanderer, reformer, and statesman. He was at the same time one of the rarest saints on earth. At his last prayer he himself observed: "This prayer is offered to my God by me, John Knox, with my half-dead tongue and perfect mind." The following are the words uttered in that prayer: "O Lord, have mercy on me. Do not judge my countless sins; forgive especially those sins which the world is not able to reprove. During the days of my youth, in the years of middle age, even up to the present

---

* The exact quotes cannot be found; therefore these and all following quoted passages have been freely translated from the Chinese texts.—*Translator*

hour, I have gone through many battles. I discover that in me there is nothing but vanity and corruption. O Lord, you alone know the secret of man's heart. Please be reminded that of the sins which I have spoken of, there is not one that I am pleased with. For them I often am sorrowful, and my inward man deeply abhors them. I now weep for my corruption; I can only rest on your mercy." This is the prayer of one who had been enlightened by God's light.

John Bunyan. For the preaching of the gospel John Bunyan was imprisoned for thirteen years. While in prison he composed what the world has come to know as *Pilgrim's Progress*, a book which has been translated into almost as many languages as has the Bible. Charles H. Spurgeon has spoken of Bunyan as follows: "I notice that John Bunyan's style is close to that of the Lord Jesus; none can surpass him." Yet, when Bunyan wrote of himself, he voiced this lament: "Since I repented last time, another matter has given me great sorrow, which is, that if I rigorously scrutinize the best of what I now do, I discover sin. New sin is mixed with my best. For this cause, I cannot but conclude that in spite of how self-conceited and imaginative I am towards myself and my work, even if my past is without blemish, the sins which I commit in one day are enough to put me in hell." And as he continued to be deeply conscious of his sin, he cried out: "If it is not because of such a great Savior, who can save such a great sinner like me?"

George Whitefield. This man was as famous a preacher as John Wesley. Near the end of his life he could say these words: "Oh, that I may collapse and die in the Lord's work, for I think He is worthy to have me die for Him. If I had a thousand bodies, each and every one of them would become a wandering preacher for Jesus' sake." When he last took a candle to retire, a large crowd gathered at his door, urging him to preach once more to them. He knew he would die that day, nonetheless he preached to them till the candle was burnt. Then he retired upstairs to die. Yet listen to what he thought of himself: "In all the duties which we fulfill there are corruptions mingled in them. Should Jesus Christ accept us according to our works after we have repented, our works would surely condemn us. For never can we offer a prayer as perfect as the moral law of God demands. I do not know how you think, but I can say: I cannot pray, I can only sin; I cannot preach to you or to other people, I can only sin. I am forced to confess: even my repentance needs to be repented of, even my tears need to be washed in the precious blood of my Redeemer. Our best works are but the refinest sins."

Augustus Toplady. In counting his sin, this most godly man had computed that were he to sin at least once every second, in ten years he would have more than three hundred million sins. He therefore wrote a most glorious hymn, which has given rest to countless numbers of weary and sin-oppressed souls. It is none other than "Rock of Ages, cleft for me, let me hide myself in thee."

Writing about himself, Toplady had this to say: "Oh, who in the world is so miserable as I am! I leave nothing but weakness and sin. There is no good in my flesh, and yet I am tempted to be highminded. The best of my work in life qualifies me for condemnation." Nevertheless, when he was dying of tuberculosis in London, he laid his sinful head upon the Savior's breast, announcing, "I am the happiest person in the whole world!"

Jonathan Edwards. This Christian was most spiritual and was greatly used by the Lord. Whenever he preached, countless numbers of people would feel pricked in their hearts, weep for their sins, and ask for the Lord's forgiveness. Being an exceedingly honest person, he most humbly wrote the following words: "Often do I sense deeply how full of sin and uncleanness I am. Due to such overwhelming feeling, frequently I cannot but cry out aloud. Sometimes I cry for a long time. For this reason, I have to shut myself up from time to time. I now sense my own wickedness and the corruption of my heart even more deeply than at the time before I repented. So far as I am concerned, I have long understood how my wickedness is wholly indestructible, having filled my thoughts and imaginations; yet at the same time I realize my sensitivity towards sin is simply too dull and loose. I myself am surprised that I do not possess greater awareness of sin. What I presently hope for most is that I may have a contrite heart so as to prostrate myself humbly before God."

David Brainerd. When David Brainerd was twenty-five years old, he labored among the poor Indians in the center of the American frontier. He toiled, suffered, prayed, and fasted till God's Spirit was poured out upon them so that many were converted and lived for the Lord. Five years later, he entered into rest.

The following are the words delivered by Jonathan Edwards at the burial of David Brainerd, his son according to the gospel: "May all God's servants and people notice this extraordinary man—he and his holiness, heavenliness, sacrificial living and labor. How he offered himself with all that he had, both in heart and in practice, to the glory of God. How steady and firm he was in all kinds of pain and sorrow under trying situations. All these serve as encouragement to us that we may know how great is the work we ought to do on earth, how lovely and precious are the experiences and conduct we have in Christ, and how admirable is the end thereof."

Yet concerning himself this servant of the Lord observed: "Alas, my inward uncleanness! Alas, my shame and iniquity before God! Alas, when I am preaching, how proud, selfish, hypocritical, ignorant, malicious, sectarian, and lacking in love, zeal, gentleness and peace I am!"

Hudson Taylor. Mr. Frost, the Canadian director of the China Inland Mission, had worked with Hudson Taylor in China for many decades. In speaking once of Mr. Taylor, Mr. Frost had this to say: "I have prayed with Mr. Taylor thousands of times, but never once did I hear him pray without confessing his sin."

All these lived closer to God than do the ordinary people, nonetheless they had such feelings as these towards themselves. May I ask the many ordinary believers among ourselves—those who have not lived as close to God and do not possess such a sense of their own corruption—are we more advanced than these great men of God? All will have to answer in the negative. Not sensing one's fault does not mean to say that one is good. Quite the contrary, this merely indicates how lacking in self-knowledge that one is. But these great men of God felt so strongly their depravity, because they were especially near to God. They received more light of God; they knew that absolute standard of His holiness. They were consequently more aware than other people of their own poverty.

Does not the first epistle of John tell us, "If we walk in the light . . . the blood of Jesus his Son cleanseth us from all sin" (1.7)? Because we are in the light, our sin is made manifest, and we then need the blood of Jesus. This is followed by, "If we say that we have no sin, we deceive ourselves, and the truth is not in us" (1.8). All who say they have no sin are self-deceived persons. The reason for such deception is that the truth—the truth which issues from God's light—is not in their heart.

Whoever is not enlightened by God's light tends to consider himself good, holy, perfect, and sinless. If we are close to God as were these great men of God, we, like them, would sense our uncleanness. For the nearer we are to God the higher our standard of holiness will become and the deeper we will recognize what uncleanness, corruption, and unrighteousness are.

The depth of our consciousness of sin is determined by the degree of God's light we receive. Many things which at the commencement of our Christian life we consider not to be sin will be recognized as in fact sinful when we grow in grace. That which in the past year was deemed to be right is now understood to be wrong because we have received more light from God during this year. What we reckon as being nothing wrong at this present moment may turn out to be so in the future when we learn more of God and His will. There is not a Christian on earth who is entirely without fault. Let us be careful lest we be deceived by the flesh into thinking we have now attained "sinless perfection."

Future Judgment

We know all Christians will in the future stand trial at the judgment seat of Christ. This judgment is not concerned with the issue of whether we are to be eternally saved or lost, rather is it for the purpose of determining whether we are able to enter the kingdom and what position we will take in the kingdom. It is concerned with how we have lived and worked daily by Christ after having been saved. Whether we will receive God's praise in the future depends on how we obey God's will today. For God is pleased with nothing apart from His own will. Of course, this matter of whether we are rewarded or not is but a small point; the real problem is whether we are able to please and to satisfy the Lord's heart. I believe every saved person shares the same desire to please the Lord, though this varies greatly in intensity.

Many believers who aspire to gain Christ often carelessly say, This or that is the will of God; or, I feel this or that is God's guidance. Beloved, do you know that for all these things we will one day be judged not according to what we say or feel or believe, but according to what the various parts of God's will really are? The third chapter of the first letter to the Corinthians tells us how we will be judged: "Each man's work shall be made manifest: for the day shall declare it, because it is revealed in fire" (verse 13). What fire is this fire? We all know the uses for fire: sometimes it is for burning, but oftentimes it is for shining. For the work of wood, hay, and stubble, fire will consume; but for the work of gold, silver, and costly stones, fire will illuminate.

We will better understand the meaning of fire if we join this 1 Corinthian verse with Revelation 1.14: "His [the Lord of judgment] eyes were as a flame of fire." At our future judgment the Lord will test our work with His fire, and His eyes are as a flame of fire. This is to say that the Lord will judge all the works we do after we are saved according to His light, that is, according to His view. His light will reveal what is of His will and what is not.

Let it be known most assuredly that before God there is but one standard for right and wrong. And this standard is absolute, unchangeable, immovable. We shall all be judged according to this standard. Whatever we may say or feel or believe or surmise today, we will suffer loss on that day if what we do is not truly according to the will of God. For in God's light nothing is hidden and nothing can be wrong. How can we stand on *that* day when God shall judge us with His light and according to His will if *today* we have not God's light to reveal to us our actual condition? If we live on earth today under God's enlightenment, knowing His will in all things, our work shall no doubt be rewarded on that day.

Let us remember that the light of God we today receive for work is the very light by which God will judge us in the future. In order to know whether or not our work can stand God's light on that day, we should ask if the work we do today is according to God's will. May I remind you that God's light never changes. What God's light condemns now as not in accordance with His will, His light will condemn in the future also as being such. What God's light approves today as being of His will will likewise be approved as being of His will in the day to come. Never run the risk of expecting reward on that day when God's light shall appear, while doing things today which are not according to God's light, God's will and God's view.

That which we daily live by is the light of God. When we say we now walk according to God's light, we mean we walk in accordance with God's judgment. Daily we walk and work with a clear view of how God will judge us in the future. Because of a good understanding of the future scene of the judgment seat, we do today what will meet His approval on that future day and refrain from doing what will on that day be condemned.

The light of God is the light of the judgment seat! Today we gain self-knowledge by God's light. By the light of the judgment seat we know and do His will. We should praise and thank God that we need not wait till that day to see God's light and to know how He will judge us, for we are able to see that light today—even now we may know what He will then condemn or approve. The Holy Spirit comes to dwell in us for the purpose of revealing to us God's light. We are therefore without excuse.

Paul too considered the future judgment of God as based on God's light. He told us how worthless it was to do things according to one's feeling. "For I know nothing against myself; yet am I not hereby justified: but he that judgeth me is the Lord. Wherefore judge nothing before the time, until the Lord come, who will both bring to light the hidden things of darkness, and make manifest the counsels of the hearts; and then shall each man have his praise from God" (1 Cor. 4.4–5).

How crystal clear is this passage. Brethren, if a person like Paul felt how untrustworthy was his own feeling, how about you and me? He concedes that apart from the shining of God's light on that day, we will have many hidden things of darkness and many counsels of the heart which could possibly influence our work. Only when the light of God shall shine on that day will we realize how much we were influenced by these hidden things. Hence, he exhorts us in the preceding verses to be faithful. For if we are faithful, that is, if we are willing to pay any cost to do God's will, God will certainly show His will to us. "If any man willeth to do his will, he shall know . . . ." (John 7.17), says the Lord Jesus.

So, brethren, let us now seek the light of God so as not to be condemned but to receive full reward in the future when this light shall appear.

A Prayer

We already know how important it is to do God's will. But if we desire to know His will, we must have a heart which wills to do His will. Our heart must be weaned from everything in order to have only one will, which is, to know His will. Whatever God reveals, be it to our view good or bad, we are willing to accept. With such a tender and submissive heart as this, God will surely reveal His will to us. For "the friendship of Jehovah is with them that fear him; and he will show them his covenant" (Ps. 25.14).

However, oftentimes we do not know our heart, nor do we realize how deceitful, crooked, and rebellious our heart is. We imagine we will obey and do God's will, but we fail to discover how in the deep recesses of our heart we are full of self-opinion. Therefore, we need to cry to God as did David: "Examine me, O Jehovah, and prove me; try my heart and my mind" (Ps. 26.2); "Search me, O God, and know my heart: try me, and know my thoughts; and see if there be any wicked way in me, and lead me in the way everlasting" (Ps. 139.23–24).

Only when God examines our thoughts do we know our thoughts; only when God tries our mind do we know our mind. After we are thus examined and tried by Him, we begin to see the wicked way in us so that we may have it removed and be led by God to walk in the everlasting way.

A great number of believers do desire to know God's will, and they also ask Him for it, yet they do not receive. This is for no other reason than that there is a wicked way in their heart. They lack self-knowledge. They do not realize how full of inclination, prejudice, fear, and lust their heart is. God is not able to reveal His will to them. If they ask God to enlighten them that they may know themselves and have all obstacles removed, then God will surely lead them. Even though self-knowledge does not automatically give us to know God's will, it shows us what is in us which hinders us from knowing His will.

Consequently, self-knowledge is indispensable in the knowing of the will of God. But who can know himself without God's light? Is this not, then, the time that we should pray the prayer of David?

PART THREE

THE RENEWING OF THE MIND

1 | The Nous

Man is a composite of spirit, soul, and body. The Bible shows us that man has a body as well as a spirit, and a soul as well as a body and a spirit. Why are the spirit and the body insufficient? Why is there also the need for a soul? It is because the soul needs to stand between the spirit and the body to serve as a medium to both. What God wishes us to know is made known to us in the intuition of our spirit; for the spirit is the organ for God-consciousness; it enables us to communicate with God and to know God. The body is given to us by God that we may be in contact with the world, thus sensing all the things in the world. But the soul is created for the purpose of self-consciousness that we may be conscious of ourselves. We human beings are not like angels who are bodiless spirits. We have a spirit and a body, together with a soul which serves as a buffer between them. In this way all which belongs to our spirit and body is being expressed through the soul.

The Human Heart

The heart, according to the Biblical concept, is the conscience of man's spirit plus the mind in man's soul. The spirit communes with God and is the organ for knowing His will, whereas the heart is the steward of the spirit, working towards the expression of all which is in the spirit. Whatever is in the spirit is expressed through the heart. The heart is therefore the link or the place of exchange for the workings of the spirit and of the soul. It is like the operating center of a telephone system where all the lines will converge and be connected. All that enters the spirit enters from the heart. Hence the heart is the connecting point of all communications. The spirit reaches the soul via the heart; and through the heart the soul conveys to the spirit what it has gathered from outside. The heart is where our personality is located. It is our real self. Since it is the link between the spirit and the soul, the heart may be considered as the real "I". Knowing the scriptural concept of the heart, we may then judge its significance to us. Let us read a few passages from the Scriptures which deal with the heart.

"Commune with your own heart upon your bed, and be still" (Ps. 4.4). In other words, the heart is myself. So that communing with one's heart suggests what is commonly known as the consultation of heart and mouth.

"Keep thy heart with all diligence; for out of it are the issues of life" (Prov. 4.24). We need to do nothing else but to keep our heart, for out of it come forth the issues of life. Whatever fruit we see in man is produced by the heart. Hence the heart is man's real self.

"Ye offspring of vipers, how can ye, being evil, speak good things? for out of the abundance of the heart the mouth speaketh. The good man out of his good treasure bringeth forth good things: and the evil man out of his evil treasure bringeth forth evil things" (Matt. 12.34–35). The Lord declares that out of the fullness of the heart does the mouth speak; for the heart is the man's own self. Whatever a sinner does comes from his heart; all sins issue from the heart.

"But the things which proceed out of the mouth come forth out of the heart; and they defile the man. For out of the heart come forth evil thoughts, murders, adulteries, fornications, thefts, false witness, railings" (Matt. 15.18–19). What springs from the heart defiles the man, for the heart is unclean.

Is it not rather surprising that though man is a composite of spirit, soul, and body, yet in regeneration God only gives us a new spirit and a new heart but not a new soul? God gives us a new spirit so that we may commune with Him by having our dead spirit quickened into functioning before Him. He also gives us a new heart so as to enable us to live a new life and to have a new desire.

Although the heart and the spirit have a number of things in common, even so, the Bible does not mix up these two but keeps them in their respective place. It is said in Ezekiel, "A new heart also will I give you, and a new spirit will I put within you; and I will take away the stony heart out of your flesh, and I will give you a heart of flesh" (36.26). God does not say, I will give you a new spirit and a new soul, for He deems the soul to be an organ not needing to be remade. Only man's heart must be recreated, because out of it flow the issues of life.

What is to be done to a believer's spirit and heart after he has sinned? "Create in me a clean heart, O God; and renew a right spirit within me" (Ps. 51.10). This verse reveals how God looks upon the heart and the spirit of a believer. If defiled, he ought to ask God to create in him a clean heart. Our heart must be clean; our spirit must be made right.

Since the Bible lays so much stress on the heart, we can see what a significant place it occupies in the Word. The heart is of exceeding importance, for it is our real self. What our heart is is what we really are. It is the source of life. It includes the conscience of the spirit and the mind of the soul. We commune with God by the spirit, but what God looks at is our heart. It is the most essential factor in our lives. We say we are saved: but how *are* we saved after all? It is when we believe in our heart. How are we now serving God? It is serving God with the heart. Whom does

God bless? Those who are upright in heart. What shall be judged in the future? God will judge the hidden things in the heart of man. For this reason, we must have a good heart when we come near to God. But a good mind is prerequisite to a good heart. And this brings us to a consideration especially of this matter of the mind or "nous".

Nous in the New Testament

The word "mind" comes from the original Greek term *nous*. It is used twenty-four times in the entire New Testament. Let us list them as follows:

> Then opened he their *mind,* that they might understand the scriptures. (Luke 24.45)
>
> And even as they refused to have God in their knowledge, God gave them up unto a reprobate *mind,* to do those things which are not fitting. (Rom. 1.28)
>
> But I see a different law in my members, warring against the law of my *mind,* and bringing me into captivity under the law of sin which is in my members. (Rom. 7.23)
>
> For who hath known the *mind* of the Lord. (Rom. 11.34)
>
> Let each man be fully assured in his own *mind.* (Rom. 14.5)
>
> But that ye be perfected together in the same *mind* and in the same judgment. (1 Cor. 1.10)
>
> For who hath known the *mind* of the Lord, that he should instruct him? But we have the *mind* of Christ. (1 Cor. 2.16)
>
> Ye no longer walk as the Gentiles also walk, in the vanity of their *mind.* (Eph. 4.17)
>
> Vainly puffed up by his fleshly *mind.* (Col. 2.18)
>
> That ye be not quickly shaken from your *mind.* (2 Thess. 2.2)

Here is the *mind* that hath wisdom. (Rev. 17.9)

I of myself with the *mind,* indeed, serve the law of God. (Rom. 7.25)

Be ye transformed by the renewing of your *mind.* (Rom. 12.2)

But my understanding [lit. *mind*] is unfruitful. (1 Cor. 14.14)

What is it then? I will pray with the spirit, and I will pray with the understanding [lit. *mind*] also: I will sing with the spirit, and I will sing with the understanding [lit. *mind*] also. (1 Cor. 14.15)

Howbeit in the church I had rather speak five words with my understanding [lit. *mind*], that I might instruct others also, than ten thousand words in a tongue. (1 Cor. 14.19)

And that ye be renewed in the spirit of your *mind.* (Eph. 4.23)

And the peace of God which passeth all understanding [lit. *mind*]. (Phil. 4.7)

Wranglings of men corrupted in *mind* and bereft of the truth. (1 Tim. 6.5)

Men corrupted in *mind,* reprobate concerning the faith. (2 Tim. 3.8)

Both their *mind* and their conscience are defiled. (Titus 1.15)

He that hath understanding [lit. *mind*], let him count the number of the beast. (Rev. 13.18)

The Relation between Nous and the Christian

What effect has this nous upon a Christian's life, work, service, walk, and so forth? It is an undeniable fact that all who believe in the Lord Jesus have a new spirit and a new heart. However weak or strong a believer may be, he is begotten of God and possesses a new spirit and a new heart. Hence he can love people from the heart as well as serve God with the heart. He is able to do everything from the heart. Yet new though his heart is, the "nous" part of it may not be renewed. According to human logic, if man's heart is made new, the conscience and mind which are included in the heart must also have been renewed. But it is not true in fact. The conscience part of the heart becomes new at the time of salvation, but it may not be always new or become daily renewed afterwards. Just as a dress when first purchased is new, it may not remain so later on. One has to perform additional work on it to keep it continually new. In like manner, the nous, at the time of salvation, is new, but after a while it may not stay new.

Such experience is shared by many believers. Let me tell you that when a person first gets saved his conscience is new and is restored to its proper function of hating and abhorring sin. But will this conscience always continue new? Not absolutely. For if he should sin and give ground to sin repeatedly, if he should refuse to listen to the voice of conscience, then after many instances of this his conscience will not reprove him any more. It has lost its function. Now just as it is possible for the conscience to be restored and then subsequently to lose its sensitivity, so is it possible for the mind.

What Is Nous?

What is this nous which the New Testament speaks of? We may view this subject from three different angles: physically viewed, we may say that we human beings possess brain; psychologically considered, we have nous; and speaking spiritually, we have intuition. That which pertains to matter is termed the brain; and that which pertains to intellect or reasoning is called nous. Though we dare not say that nous represents the whole of the mind, it certainly occupies a major part of the mind nonetheless. Through the intuition of our spirit we receive an impression from God. By the nous of the soul that impression in the intuition is being interpreted and made known to us. We know the will of God through intuition, but intuition, being unrational and unsystematic, needs to be explained by the nous.

Now let us further say that man has three different organs for knowledge. In the body is the brain, in the spirit is the intuition, and in the soul is the nous. When we dissect the brain, we see nothing but the gray and white substance. And intuition is something which we sometimes sense and sometimes do not sense. At times it seems to constrain, at other times it seems to restrain. It is that entity which is deep down in us. But the nous stands between the intuition and the brain. It interprets the meaning in the intuition and directs the brain to express it in words. Should a believer's nous be defective, and even though he has strong intuition and a good brain, his life will be lived devoid of any standard. He will spend his days foolishly. And he will not be able to express what is within him, even at the time of preaching. All this is due to his nous not being renewed.

The Sinner's Nous

Let us first consider the nous of a sinner. He has a nous which is corrupted and depraved (Rom. 1.28, 2 Tim. 3.8), futile and vain (Eph. 4.17), fleshly (Col. 2.18), and defiled (Titus 1.15). Such is the condition of a sinner's nous. But now you are saved. Yet if you recall your experience before you were saved, what could be said of your attitude towards God? What is the situation of a sinner's nous before Him?

Suppose that here is a most foolish sinner who knows almost nothing. But as you start to talk to him about God, he will oppose you with all sorts of arguments. He will insist that there is no God. You will be surprised at this assertion of a fool. Why does he so speak? Because his mind is darkened. His nous is darkened and dead; his spirit is completely in the dark. He has no way to know God and is totally unable to understand the way of God. What makes him raise all these arguments against God? His depraved, futile and defiled nous. Such is the situation of the foolish man.

But how about the cleverest of men, the one who can discuss God philosophically? He professes to know everything, yet he will not believe in God. He tries to find many reasons to refute Him. He opposes God as much as the fool. Though the wise and the fool are worlds apart in hundreds of things, in the matter of not believing in God they perfectly agree. This is due to no other cause than that the nous in both of them is darkened and their spirit is dead. Their nous being dead, they are unable to receive the light of God. Their thoughts become wild and irregular. Hence, God declares in the case of those perishing that "the god of this world hath blinded the minds of the unbelieving, that the light of the gospel of the glory of Christ, who is the image of God, should not dawn upon them" (2 Cor. 4.4).

Nous and Salvation

What is meant by being saved? It simply means knowing God. "And this is life eternal, that they should know thee the only true God, and him whom thou didst send, even Jesus Christ" (John 17.3). Eternal life is the ability of knowing God. Being saved does not mean one can talk about certain doctrines; it is having a living knowledge of God. Should we ask the most intelligent and learned man in the world to converse with a young believer who is newly saved, the first man may raise hundreds of arguments to oppose God and to which the second man has no answer. Nevertheless, the young believer can say, I know I have eternal life, I know I am saved. Such is the difference between them. The nous of an unbeliever is blocked; it is in lack of light. But at the moment he is saved, his nous receives light, thus knowing God. Many have their eyes opened when they hear the powerful gospel for the first time. They know they are sinners and they know Jesus Christ is their Savior. Though they are still unable to explain intelligently their experience, they nonetheless do have the knowledge of knowing that they have been enlightened and that they are now saved. This knowing is the work of the nous.

What God has given to our intuition is communicated to the brain through the nous. To the spiritual, as soon as there is the movement of God in his intuition it is instantly registered in his nous and carried out by his brain. Upon our being saved we possess a special kind of knowledge that we may know God. Intuition, nous, and brain work jointly and simultaneously. Only for the sake of clarity have we described them separately.

2 | The Renewing of the Nous

Our nous is enlightened at the time we are saved. Often we assume that a new heart is enough for us, not knowing that the Bible says our nous needs to be renewed too. Even though our nous becomes new at regeneration, has it been renewed forever afterwards? I am afraid the nous of many saved ones has not been renewed. Things remain the same as before conversion.

I must say frankly that the thoughts in many believers today are not very different from that of sinners. How frequently I have the feeling that though the spirit and the heart of many believers are new, their nous lacks renewal and acts like that of sinners. How can a believer expect to be of any use in God's hand if his nous has not been renewed? Our nous must not only be new but also be daily renewed.

Today's defect lies here: at the moment we are saved we receive a tremendous revelation, yet after being saved our nous is not renewed. Salvation becomes the greatest revelation of our lives, but do we continuously receive other great revelations subsequently? I am afraid many do not have any further great revelations after that of salvation. The revelation of salvation is without question the greatest revelation in life for it brings us into eternity; but do we experience other new revelations?

Why is it that because of the enlightenment of our first believing in the Lord we are able to confess our sins, to brave persecutions, to endure opposition from relatives as well as from the world, and to forsake the world? Oh, it is because this nous has enabled us to know salvation and to live in newness of life. And were the light of this nous to shine in our lives *daily,* we would live a life of true enlightenment all along the way.

There was once a woman who loved the world most dearly. She could not forsake it for anything. One day she heard a man preaching in the church hall. The preaching was in no way exceptional, but the Scripture he read was as follows: "And this is the victory that hath overcome the world, even our faith" (1 John 5.4). This word captured her heart. She heard that man mention this word seven or eight times. Never before did she know what the world was, but that day she saw through the world. She crushed it to pieces on the very same day. Such knowing as this is the knowledge of the nous.

Many are unable to cast things off because their nous lacks the light to see through these things. In addition, if our nous does not cooperate, our hearing the Word and our service will be of no avail. Every time we hear the Word we need the cooperation of the nous. Before we are saved we refuse to believe, in spite of strong persuasion. But one day we believe because our nous begins to know, and that we cannot overturn. Knowing the only true God and knowing Jesus Christ whom God has sent—this is eternal life.

The Conditions of the Unrenewed Nous

What are the conditions of an unrenewed nous? We may view them from three sides: towards men, towards God, and towards self. We shall see how an unrenewed nous affects man in his attitude and reaction in these three directions.

1. The unrenewed nous towards men.

If a person's nous is not renewed he will have very inaccurate ideas about others. A strange attitude which emerges is that he can never trust anybody. He is always suspicious. All the observations which come out from him are critical and hair-splitting. He inclines to denigrate other people's worth. Simply by asking myself how I think of others a person can pretty much assess the state of his nous. The Bible reveals that the Lord Jesus never judges by what His eyes see and His ears hear, for He always decides everything by His spiritual sense. How nowadays, though, believers judge others on the basis of sight and sound! If we would test everything as Paul did, we would be much happier. There is a verse in Philemon which is most precious: "hearing of thy love, and of the faith which thou hast toward the Lord Jesus, and toward all the saints" (verse 5). If any believer lowers the value of others, his nous is unquestionably defective. Let us therefore ask ourselves: Do we always devalue other people?

I knew a brother who had the habit of estimating gifts given him at lower than their original price. For example, if someone gave him a gift which was worth two dollars, he would estimate it as being worth only thirty cents. Or if he was given a thirty-dollar gift, he would declare its value to be only a little more than ten dollars. Innumerable believers think in the same way. Why? Because their nous is old and worldly. People of this world always think poorly of others. Others are suspected of harboring unuttered words behind the words actually spoken, just like meat which is enclosed in dumplings. Christians ought not think this way. If they do, it just proves that their nous is not yet renewed; and so Satan can work in their mind, because an unrenewed nous serves as an operation center for the enemy. Whatever belongs to Adam becomes natural ground for Satanic working.

2. The unrenewed nous towards God.

By noticing the following characteristics, the unrenewed nous of a believer may be detected. He is unable to put his trust in God nor is he able to know God as he has once known the Lord Jesus as his Savior. He is full of doubts. He doubts the power, the wisdom, and the love of God. These three points summarize his attitude towards God. He doubts God's power, wondering if He is able; he doubts God's wisdom, thinking He might be wrong; and he doubts God's love, musing that He is not willing.

Moreover, this believer cannot understand the Bible nor God's teaching. His nous is obstructed; he is unable to receive God's light therein. Actually, he was enlightened at the time he was saved. And had his nous been opened daily to God thereafter, he today would not be so powerless and so tense as he is.

If all of us had an unveiled nous, we would receive much light. Our nous is defective if we ourselves do not receive something new from God but can only pass on that which we have received from others. I do not say that we should not have others to help us. I myself am most happy to receive help from other people. I only say that if we are not able to receive something directly from God, our nous is defective. Our nous must be enlightened by God, and then our message will in turn enlighten the nous of other people and really help them. It is for this reason that I have said that each one himself needs to receive something from God in his nous.

One whose nous is not renewed does not know the will of God. He may reach his conclusion by means of logic, but he is unable to know God's will with his nous. He ought to know the will of God, just as at the time of salvation he knew Christ as the Son of God as well as he knew himself to be a saved person. Knowing God's will should be an inward knowledge. Oftentimes we know it but are unable to explain it. If a newly-believing country peasant is brought before an unbelieving intellectual, he may be subjected to hours of attack upon his faith without his knowing how to refute the assault, yet the believing peasant can still say he knows he is saved. This is the way of knowing God's will.

Today so many people do not know the will of God. I conclude that it is due to a deficiency in the organ for knowing God's will. The Lord's Day is considered the busiest one in the radio industry. Many large church groups in Europe and America broadcast their sermons. These radio waves reach far and wide. Why is it that we here in China do not hear them? The only reason is the lack of powerful enough radio receivers. In like manner, the will of God is most distinct and clear, but due to a deficiency in the organ for receiving it some are unable to know His will. I have said before that a believer is capable of knowing God's will just as he is able to distinguish wheat from tares. Why, then, do some not know? Due to their lack of a renewed nous.

What about our thoughts? They are corrupted. After we are saved, we Christians concede that we should have good hearts. We offend God if we have any hate or sin in our heart. We thus remind ourselves to always keep the heart from error. But we forget that our thoughts must also be good. Are our minds, our speech, our concern and outlook the same as before we were saved? I do not wish to probe into the motive and intent of the heart. I only ask if our mind has undergone a change. How strange that after we are saved our mind is as confused as before. There is no change in our speech and thought. If we do not overcome in thought, we will be thoroughly defeated.

Once a sister wrote to another sister: "If Satan can seize our thought life, he will capture all of our life." This is a fact. For such a word is spoken out of more than fifty years of deep experience before God. Brethren, think not that good intention is enough. If our thought and our evaluation towards men and events remain unchanged after we are saved, we are still in the grip of the enemy and have no way to overcome Satan.

3. The unrenewed nous towards self.

(a) *Cannot control our thoughts.* To those who have an unrenewed nous, they have absolutely no control over their own thought. Many Christians have wasted their power of thinking. If our hands can do only eight hours of work but these hours are spent in doing irregular things, we are not only wasting our strength—we are neglecting our regular work as well. Similarly, if we squander our mental power on meaningless and improper things we will not be able to think on the right things. One brother asked me why he could not concentrate. He said that after praying for five minutes his mind began to roam. I asked him in return if his thought wandered only in prayer or did this happen throughout the day? I could answer for him that his thoughts must have been scattered and must have wandered around the world during the whole day. How then could he concentrate in prayer when his mind was so confused during the twelve hours of the day? He was not able to conceive one good thought from morning till night. Consequently, a believer whose nous is not renewed is unable to control his thought. May I therefore say emphatically that such a one is not of much use in God's hand. To become good believers, Christians need to have their nous renewed.

(b) *Introspective.* One of the greatest ills in a believer is to be introspective. He may fancy introspection as good, but it never really helps him to know himself. No one ever arrives at self-knowledge by looking inwardly into himself. Self-knowledge comes only through God's light. It is in His light that we see light (see Ps. 36.9). All self-criticism and self-analysis, whether it commends or condemns self, will bring unrest to the mind. It will not be right for me to secretly compare myself to other people. Each time a believer looks into himself his progress is arrested. Just imagine how one would have to stand still if he desired to look at himself while walking. He cannot proceed on his way and at the same time look at himself. All who turn to look at themselves will either become immobilized or turn backwards. This is especially true in spiritual progress. Whoever turns inwardly upon himself will become greatly discouraged. He will put himself in danger if there is no one to help him on. He may even imagine that he has not been saved or that he has committed the unpardonable sin. He may be deceived into surmising that God has forsaken him. Such will be the consequence of an unrenewed nous.

(c) *Unable to communicate God's word.* If our nous is not renewed we will not be able to impart to other people what God has given us. Some believers are quite conversational. They have the right words for hundreds of matters which they enjoy explaining or describing. They may be called eloquent. But when the conversation turns upon spiritual matters they are unable to elucidate even one of them. Why is this so? It is because their mind is not usable to God. Their mind is as weak as a child's arm which cannot lift ten pounds. Although they may have many thoughts, their thoughts are so confused that they do not know which come from God and which do not. They themselves understand what they have received intuitively, but they do not possess the ability to interpret their intuitive knowledge and communicate to others. All this is due to the lack of renewal in their nous. God will of course give utterance if He wishes people to speak His word. Still, without a renewed nous none can express what he has inwardly received.

A believer needs a renewed nous to guide him in his daily walk. Otherwise he will suffer a great deal of loss. He may misunderstand people; he may not know God's will; and he may even misuse himself. And so he is not able to live well. Hence we all must seek to experience this step of the renewing of the nous. All the people of this world are divided into the saved and the unsaved, the regenerated and unregenerated, those who are in Christ and those who are in Adam. Such difference is absolute and distinctive. Likewise, the nous of all believers can be divided into the renewed and the unrenewed. And this difference is also clearly defined. Being saved, we need to have our nous renewed—and not just önce, but renewed daily.

Once Dwight L. Moody was walking on the street. He suddenly requested a homeowner to permit him to use his upper room. He was given permission. Moody went to the upper room and prayed, "Oh God, stay your hand, for it is more than I can bear." If we have our nous daily renewed, we shall find that what God has given to our nous is more than we can contain. Let me say again that this renewing of the nous is to be specifically sought after just as we have in the past sought for new birth. Just as new birth has changed our life, so this renewed nous shall transform our daily living.

Do not think that the naturally clever person progresses faster in the knowledge of God than the naturally dull. If spiritual progress is to be measured by natural wisdom the whole thing falls into the realm of the flesh. Your progress has nothing to do with your natural wisdom. If your nous has been renewed, you will be able to know God and the things of God; the cleverest person beside you may not comprehend what you have comprehended. Consequently, seek earnestly for the renewing of your nous, else you will not be able to carry on spiritually.

Before you were saved you did not love people. Yet now since you have believed in the Lord you make great strides in loving them. If such a phenomenon fails to appear, I doubt whether you are really saved. If you are truly saved, you will be different with respect to such matters as loving people, being patient, and serving others from the heart. Formerly you liked to be great, now you are willing to bear and forbear. All this is due to your having a new heart. Other people will also notice your change. They will acknowledge that you are different from what you were before. Nonetheless, I would ask you if your mind is also transformed? Are you more able to concentrate and to think systematically? Or does your mind remain unchanged? Should the latter be the case, this indicates that your nous has not been renewed.

A believer, be he wise or dull, ought to have a better nous as well as a better heart. God is no respecter of persons. He will destroy the wisdom of the wise and set aside the cleverness of the clever. He puts the wise and the dull on the same footing. The nous of the wise needs renewal as much as the nous of the dull. Only after your nous is renewed will you be able to know God and His will and to see and interpret what He has shown you. Thus will you advance in the course which lies ahead of you.

Indeed, the difference between a renewed and an unrenewed nous is as the difference between a shiny glass window and a dirty glass window. The unrenewed nous of a believer is unable to think and to do what the renewed nous is capable of thinking and doing. His renewed nous will increase at least several times its thinking capability. Its power of thinking will be greatly improved. So that the difference between a renewed nous and an unrenewed one is as the difference between life and death, heaven and earth. Were we to deal with our nous in the same fervor as once we sought salvation, we would live under an open heaven.

3 | The Nous and the Spirit

God communicates with us in our spirit, not through our soul and body. We ought to maintain an open and sensitive spirit before Him in order to maintain living communication with Him. But what we are concerned with now is the relationship between our spirit and the nous. Whenever there is a closed nous there is a closed spirit. If the nous is closed, God's light will not be imparted to the spirit, for there will be no outlet for whatever the spirit may obtain. In other words, if the mind of a Christian is defective, his spirit will follow suit. Not so with the body. A Christian may be ill physically, yet his sickness may not affect his spirit. Many Christians lie in bed throughout the year; even so, they are still able to sense God's will, to be obedient to Him, and to do the work of prayer. But when a Christian's nous is impaired his spirit will invariably be marred, for the first has an instant effect on the second.

There are two passages in the Bible which tell us of the need of having our nous renewed. Without its renewal we believers will find it difficult to go on with the Lord. Let us look at the first of these two passages, the second of which we shall deal with in the next chapter.

> This I say therefore, and testify in the Lord, that ye no longer
> walk as the Gentiles also walk, in the vanity of their mind,
> being darkened in their understanding, alienated from the life
> of God, because of the ignorance that is in them, because of
> the hardening of their heart; who being past feeling gave
> themselves up to lasciviousness, to work all uncleanness with
> greediness. But ye did not so learn Christ; if so be that ye
> heard him, and were taught in him, even as truth is in Jesus:
> that ye put away, as concerning your former manner of life,
> the old man, that waxeth corrupt after the lusts of deceit; and
> that ye be renewed in the spirit of your mind, and put on the
> new man, that after God hath been created in righteousness
> and holiness of truth. (Eph. 4.17–24)

Nous is twice mentioned in this passage, and this is what we
will take note of. The word "understanding" in verse 18 in the
original is *dianoia;* it comes from the same root in Greek as *nous,*
with a slight variation. What is the difference between *nous* and
noia? Nous is the organ, while noia is the function—just as the eye is
an organ while seeing is its function. Hence verse 17 speaks of the
nature of this organ of nous, but verse 18a describes the condition
of its functioning.

"Alienated from the life of God, because of the ignorance that
is in them, because of the hardening of their heart" (verse 18). The
heart here is our real self, our very personality.

"Who being past feeling" (verse 19). It means being numbed,
that is, insensitive. Such a term is often used medically. All physi-
cians will tell us that some wounds can be so painful that they may
reach the point of numbness in the patients. Though their wounds
are still putrifying, they no longer sense the pain. Similarly, people's hearts can be so hardened as to be void of any feeling.

"That ye put away, as concerning your former manner of life,
the old man, that waxeth corrupt after the lusts of deceit" (verse

22). This means that having heard the truth in Jesus, you have already put off your old man. Hence you should do what is described from verse 25 onward.

"That ye be renewed in the spirit of your mind" (verse 23). This continues to tell what the believers have already possessed in Christ according to the truth in Jesus. We not only have put off the old man but we also have the spirit of our nous constantly renewed. The spirit of our nous needs constant renewal just as the old man is forever corrupting.

"Put on the new man, that after God hath been created in righteousness and holiness of truth" (verse 24). This contrasts with verse 22. It also tells us of what is factual in the Lord. Thus verses 22 to 24 speak of the accomplished facts we have in Christ, whereas from verse 25 onward there is the charge as to how we should conduct ourselves hereafter.

This passage therefore shows us three important things: our spiritual life, our heart, and our nous.

The Heart Is First Corrupted

Let us now concentrate on what verses 17 and 18 say. The nous of the Gentiles is vain, and the heart is so corrupted that it has no more feeling. But how does all this begin? If we know in what part corruption has its start, we will be able to deal with that particular part. Is it the nous of man, the life of man, or the heart of man which is first corrupted? If the root of all ills is found to be the heart, then we will deal first with the heart; if it is the nous, then let us deal first with the nous; and if it is the life, then we must deal first with the life.

The two verses reveal the order of our fall. The apostle exhorts the believers not to walk as the Gentiles, who walk in the vanity of their nous. (This vain nous is what is commonly termed "building castles in the air.") Why should we not so walk? Because their "noia" (understanding) is darkened. Why is their noia darkened? Because they are alienated or excluded from the life of God. And why is their life alienated from the life of God? Because of the ignorance in them, the hardness of their heart. Consequently, we discover that the disease begins with the heart.

It is due to the hardening of the heart that life is alienated from God, and because of the alienation from the life of God the noia is darkened. Brothers and sisters, all the corruption of man is in the heart. I often tell my fellow-workers that it is the heart, not the head, which is corrupted. People usually think it is man's head which is so; but I say no, it is the heart which is corrupted.

The Gentiles will not believe in their hearts. Do you know why Gentiles will not believe in the Lord Jesus but will raise up many arguments instead? Is it because we do not have good reasons for them to believe in God and in Christ? Not at all. We have very good reasons. But the psalmist says, "The fool hath said in his *heart*, There is no God" (Ps. 14.1). It is not that his mind is inadequate, but that his heart says there is no God. The Lord Jesus told the Jews when they did not believe in Him, "Ye do not wish to come to me, that ye may have life" (John 5.40 literal). It is a matter of the heart, not of reasoning. It is the heart which will not believe.

Some people give assent to the many reasons I give them as to why there is a God and why the Lord Jesus is the Savior, yet they do not then believe in God and in the Lord Jesus. This proves that the heart, not the head, is wrong. It is for this reason that Paul says that "with the heart man believeth unto righteousness" (Rom. 10.10). The Lord Jesus tells us that whoever does "not doubt in his heart, but shall believe that what he saith cometh to pass; he shall have it" (Mark 11.23). The head is not the real problem; it is enough if the heart believes. This heart is our real self, our personality. Hence the Bible speaks of an "evil heart of unbelief" (Heb. 3.12); it does not speak of a wicked unbelieving head. It is the heart, not the head, which is corrupted. Thus the Gentiles will not believe unto salvation. Man's nous is darkened because his heart is what is *first* corrupted.

A Christian's Heart and His Nous

This is true not only of the Gentiles; it is also true with the Christian. Many Christians do not know God's will, cannot obey Him and are unable to understand the Bible simply because something is wrong with their hearts. A defective nous is but a symptom; a wrong heart is the cause of that symptom. I do not say the nous is entirely free from ailment, but here I wish to emphasize that the heart must be sick first. If the heart is corrected, the function of the nous will also be corrected. It is futile to deal with the symptom; it is effective only when the cause is touched. Let us now briefly consider a few instances in which we can see that if the heart is corrected, a defective nous will be made right.

(1) *In the matter of obedience.* Let us for example take up the issue of baptism. The Holy Scriptures have given us clear and exact revelation on baptism. Yet why is it that many believers do not act in obedience to the teaching of the Scriptures but raise up many opposing views instead? The cause lies in the heart, not in the head. Upon hearing a message on how baptism is scriptural and is that which God has distinctly asked people to do, a believer should go to God praying, "O God, if this thing is of you, I am willing to obey." As he searches the Bible he shall know God's will and obey Him. But what if another believer dismisses this as nonsense after he has heard? Even if he should read the pertinent Scripture passages afterwards, he will not understand. For when he listens to anyone preaching this truth, his is the reaction of a lawyer in the court. The first thought of a lawyer is how to refute the other party. He does not inquire if the opposite party has good reason; he only drills in his reason. Hence many questions are raised through a wrong motive of the heart.

(2) *In the matter of listening to a message.* In listening to a message, when we hear being preached something different from what we believe, we should ask God whether what is preached is wrong; if it is not, then we should inquire of Him as to the reason *we* are mistaken. Our hearts are right if we are able to be humble and teachable before God. Even though our thoughts may be misled for a time, that will soon be corrected. But if our hearts are otherwise inclined—we wish only to argue—then we will find one or two verses in the Bible to oppose what is preached to us. Many Christians read their Bible as lawyers study the law. They aim at protecting their own interests. So that it is again the heart and not the head which is wrong. And not because they cannot think, but because their hearts are already evilly inclined. Thus they drag their minds as well as their whole beings into the danger zone. .

(3) *In the matter of studying the Bible.* Are there brothers and sisters in our midst who have the brains yet do not know the Bible? I say, we do not know the Bible because our hearts are defective; for the Holy Spirit will guide us into all the truths. I wonder why some people cannot understand the Scriptures. If it is not because of the wrong inclination of their heart, what else can it be? Some perhaps are too subjective to have the light of God's word shine upon their nous. Nonetheless, it is the heart which is first corrupted, because the nous follows suit. A prejudiced heart corrupts the mind.

Some have suggested that the fall of Eve recorded in Genesis 3 did not start at the moment she ate the forbidden fruit but began instead with her wrong heart desire. So that when she was talking with Satan, her heart was already dissatisfied with God and hence already corrupted. Genesis 6 therefore states that "Jehovah saw that the wickedness of man was great in the earth, and that every imagination of the thoughts of his heart was only evil continually" (verse 5). The nous is evil because the heart is first corrupted.

A brother once pointed out that before Eve ate the forbidden fruit she had already fallen. For in her conversation with Satan she added "neither shall ye touch it" to the word of God. This indicates that her heart was already evilly inclined. God did not say the imagination of man's thoughts was evil till in Genesis 6. For it is the heart which first is evilly inclined, next man is alienated from the life of God, and finally his imagination and thoughts are corrupted. A Christian whose heart is right is able to receive God's light from the Bible, to easily know the will of God, and to obtain from Him the most abundant grace.

(4) *In the matter of listening to others.* By holding conversation with a person one may detect whether that person's mind is right or wrong. The one who is able to listen has a sound mind. The mind of certain Christians is like a wheel which endlessly rotates all day long. He is not able to listen to, and absorb, what people have said to him; his mind will only raise questions rather than receive the truth. Such a condition proves that his mind is wrong. And a wrong mind simply shows a diseased heart. Sometimes a person likes to cut in during conversations and cut off other people's words. This too reveals a heart full of problems. Now even though it is allowable occasionally to cut in and to add a word or two during conversation to express approval or disapproval, the one who *frequently* does this shows evidence of serious heart trouble.

Your nous must be defective if the thoughts of your head rotate unceasingly all the day through. In such a condition, you are unable to hear what God says to you or what other people say to you. And the reason for this sickness lies in your heart. It is because you have a heart of self-complacency, self-reliance, or self-cleverness. Harboring preconceived thoughts, naturally you are not able to hear another's words. This disability of hearing is a symptom of a defective nous which in turn is due to a wrong heart.

We know that whatever we have heard from the outside has to be delivered to the inside. Only in this way shall we ever understand what is heard. Such work of delivering or conveying is similar to doing translation. If a person does not understand the English he has heard, he needs someone to translate it into Chinese. And this translation work takes place very quickly within us. Now in case a person does not understand what he has heard, it is due to the failure of the nous to translate. If he has heard and heard wrongly, it shows that the nous has interpreted wrongly.

Once I was preaching at a certain place. I told the audience that we were saved by what Christ had accomplished for us, not by our own works. In the audience were two Taoists who told others afterwards that what I had preached was nothing but persuading people to do good. Many cannot accept God's word because their inside is already filled to capacity. They will never be able to understand the word of God if what is already within is not cleared out. Our heart before God must be like an infant's—humbly teachable. Our prayer ought to be: "O God, I do not know whether the word preached is good or bad, right or wrong. I only ask that you give me a judgment that I may know what is right and what is wrong." With such an attitude we shall see what God wants us to see. Many think they do not understand the truth because their mind is inadequate, not realizing that the root cause is their wrong heart.

(5) *In the matter of thoughts.* Some minds think too much while some are too vacuous. At times people are too keen to think; at other times they are too dull to do any thinking at all. In general, the mind of a Christian is in either of these two states. If it is not turning endlessly in thought, then it is without any thought whatsoever. Some believers are so poor in memory that they depend on their written memoranda by which to live. I personally am not against using memos, but if a believer has to depend on such a device daily to help him remember, something is wrong with his mind. Believers should not be slaves to their memo pads, so said

Jessie Penn-Lewis. Now of course, we all sometimes forget. Certain things do not leave very deep impressions on our mind and therefore they are soon forgotten. This is natural. But should the impression be deep enough and still we cannot remember, something must be wrong.

Unable to remember and overly forgetful are both abnormal states. Any person who cannot think is defective in his mind. Except we are paralyzed, we can use our hands and feet. In like manner, unless the mind is sick we ought to be able to use it. A person becomes passive in his mind if he cannot think anything voluntarily but has to be ordered to do so by outside people. A believer's mind is sick if he is unable to think; his mind is equally sick if he *always* thinks. An inability to initiate thinking and an inability to stop thinking are both improper. The minds of some are so dull through bondage that they cannot think of anything; while the minds of others are so active that they cannot call a halt at all to their thinking. Both alike are sick.

The Danger of an Unrenewed Nous

I have briefly mentioned only some of the symptoms of a sick nous. All of these can be traced to the heart. Many find their mind dull and despondent because their heart is lazy. It is similar to patients who love to be sick after a long period of illness. They would rather be ill than to arise and work. When a person's mind is tired and overworked, he can no longer think. He needs proper rest. But if he never likes to work, it reveals how lazy his heart must be. Thinking too much or thinking not at all is evidence of a defective nous, which in turn is evidence of a wrong heart.

In Ephesians 4 the apostle declares that due to the hardening of their hearts, the Gentiles are alienated from the life of God, and God's light is unable to shine upon their nous. Without the light of

God's life, their nous becomes vain and the functioning of their nous is darkened. But their nous falls into such a terrible state because their heart is hardened. Such is the situation of the Gentiles. The danger which believers face before God is to fall into the same predicament as have the Gentiles.

4 | The Way of Renewing

We will now ask ourselves, How can the nous be renewed? We have a new life; we have a new heart; our nous has been renewed and enlightened by God at least once. Our present need is to have our nous open to God daily to receive all which is of Him, to know His will, to comprehend His heart, and to understand His teaching. Brethren, do you want to know God's will? God's heart? the teaching of the Bible? If you really desire this, your nous must be renewed.

In our passage from Ephesians, the apostle instructs us that, having heard Him and having been taught the truth in Jesus, we must practice what we have learned. Therefore the exhortations from verse 25 onward are all based on the teaching of verses 20 to 24. In other words, verses 20 to 24 show us the position which a Christian has in the Lord, while the verses from 25 onward tell us of the conduct which a Christian who possesses such a position must have in the world. So far as *fact* goes, we in the Lord have already put off the old man; but this does not mean that in *experience* we will no more see the shadow of the old man. Positionally, our nous is already made new; but this too does not imply that our mind does not need to be continually renewed. On the contrary, the renewing of the nous is a constant need.

Put Away the Old Man

"Put away, as concerning your former manner of life, the old man, that waxeth corrupt after the lusts of deceit; and that ye be renewed in the spirit of your mind" (Eph. 4.22–23). The spirit of the nous shows the special relation between the nous and the spirit. In order for the spirit of our nous to be renewed we need to put away the old man. If we have not experientially put away the old man, we will not be able to experience the continual renewing of the mind.

Putting away the old man is something specific. If a believer wishes to ask himself whether or not his nous is renewed, he need only ask whether he has once irrevocably put away, as concerns his manner of life, the old man and put on the new man. Accordingly, this passage shows us that we must put away the old man specifically if we wish to have our mind and nous renewed. And to assure continual renewal, there needs to be a persistent putting away of the old man. Just as in undressing ourselves we decide to lay aside our clothes, so we must exercise our will to cast the old man away. Whatever belongs to the old man, be it word or thought or act, must be continually rejected. Whether it is sin or uncleanliness or self, it needs to be denied. On the other hand, we must also ask definitely and trust wholeheartedly that the Holy Spirit would renew our nous. This renewing of the nous is the work of the Holy Spirit. If we get rid of the obstacle by putting away the old man and then trust the Holy Spirit for the work of renewing, He will do it for us.

I wish to draw your attention to one thing. What is said in Romans 6 concerning the old man is different from what is said here. Romans 6 speaks of the accomplished fact in the Lord, saying that our old man was crucified. Thus it requires us to reckon, that is to say, to believe. Here, however, it does not deal with the fact of having been crucified; instead it considers the fact of putting away. Having been crucified is something to believe, hence it is a matter of *faith*. Putting away on the other hand is a matter of *will*. For us to put away something it requires us to exercise the will. We must therefore not only believe that our old man was crucified but also cast aside this old man of ours with a special show of our will. It will not be successful if we merely have the faith but not the will to put away the old man. Will is as necessary as our faith.

Deal with Sin in the Heart

Another thing should also be noticed: since all defects of the nous come from the heart of man, a prejudiced heart must be corrected before the nous can be renewed. An abnormal heart can hinder the light of God. Just as a leaf may block out the light, so a little sin can cover up God's light. Many have had sin in their hearts. With such sin properly dealt with, the heart turns right and the believer may thereafter know the will of God. Anyone who does not know God's will finds his heart being corrupted first.

Who is the man whom God can teach? The one who is willing to say to Him, "O God, I thank You if You will teach me now; but even if You will not teach me at this moment, I am willing to let it pass." He who is teachable before God will, when he listens to a message, inquire of God in this manner: "O God, am I wrong? Is what is preached right?" Listening to a message can very well test the correctness of the heart.

What is most precious in a renewed nous is that it may either open or close your thought. A renewed nous is able, as to God, to know God's will; is able, as to self, to control one's own thought; is able, as to others, to discuss and to understand what is said.

Put On the New Man

"And put on the new man, that after God hath been created in righteousness and holiness of truth" (verse 24). This refers to positive conduct. If we wish to have a renewed nous and have it always renewed, we need to put on the new man experimentally. This, too, is an act of will. What is meant by putting on the new man? Our new man is created in righteousness and holiness of truth according to the image of God. In short, the characteristics of this new man are righteousness and holiness of truth. Righteousness pertains to the way of God, while holiness refers to God's nature.

God is known in three different aspects: glory, holiness, and righteousness. Glory points to God himself, holiness refers to God's nature, and righteousness indicates His way of doing things. It is quite true that we are created in God's image; but this is restricted to God's righteousness and holiness. We cannot share in God's glory, since glory is His Divinity; but we shall have God's holiness and righteousness. For us to be like Him we must let God's nature work in us and work according to His way.

How many believers today have a deep sense of sin? I am ashamed to confess that my sensitivity towards sin is not deep enough. Miss Barber was one who really knew what sin is and what the holiness of God is. You might be proud and jealous all your life without ever realizing what pride and jealousy actually were until you came before this sister. You would then become aware of what you had before been unconscious of. She hated sin most vehemently and dealt with it most skillfully. Since she was so intensely strict with herself, she could be most candid with others. As soon as you came into her presence you were made to see what pride and jealousy in fact were. This sister really knew God. Many times we may not learn the truth from what is preached but we do learn it from what is lived.

If you pass over a sin the first time, and the next time, and the time after that, you will lose the sense of sin. But if you call sin a sin and deal with it properly in the first instance, you will be able to deal with it in the next. All who do not know what sin is do not know what holiness is. For holiness is the knowledge of sin. Before

Adam and Eve sinned, their status was neutral, not holy. Only by knowing sin were they brought to understand the meaning of holiness.

What is unrighteousness? What ought not be done is unrighteousness. I did not know what unrighteousness was till I read a story in the paper. A certain man went to hear another man preach in the church. When the preacher finished his message he came down from the platform and sat by him. But in getting to his seat, the preacher unwittingly stepped on the raincoat belonging to a lady in the first row. He kicked it aside without trying to wipe off the dirt, nor did he apologize to the owner of the raincoat. The other man offered a judgment on the incident by saying how unrighteous the preacher was. What is unrighteousness? It is owing people something. If you will not repay the lady, you should at least try to clean the coat for her; otherwise you will always owe her something before God.

In view of this, our nous is closely related to our life before God. Whenever we pass over a sin we are unrighteous. We cannot commune with God and at the same time our nous be darkened. Believers ought, on the negative side, to put away all uncleanness, perverse intention, and unrighteousness, and ought, on the positive side, to put on the new man. Brethren, we must pass through this door. The renewal of the nous is something which we have to deal with specifically. Do not think that we will grow into it gradually.

The Relationship between Nous and Spirit

Quite some years ago I read in a magazine these words written by Jessie Penn-Lewis: "If your spirit is closed, it is because your nous is closed." In other words, the spirit is closed due to a closed nous. At that time I knew immediately how precious were these words, though I did not see their accuracy until later because of the shallowness of my spiritual life then. It is quite true that a person's spirit is closed if his nous is closed, because spirit expresses its thought through the nous. If the nous is blocked, the spirit will have no outlet.

We may use the electric current as an example. Powerful though it may be, the current cannot give light to people if the filament in the electric bulb is broken. It is not that the power company produces no electricity; not at all; it is simply because the current cannot extend itself out through the bulb. Even so, if our nous is closed, the spirit has no way and no power to express itself. I really do not know how I should speak so as to help us into this deep truth that we may receive the renewing of our nous.

I do not suggest that our mind may help in God's work, for this will only be the power of the soul. I must say, however, that if a believer's nous is not renewed his spirit has no way out, and accordingly God cannot use him. Peter explained that the disciples on the day of Pentecost were not drunk at all. If they were drunk their minds would not be clear; and if their minds were not clear they would not have open spirits and so be used of God. So far as I know, all who are greatly used by God are people whose spirit, nous, understanding, thought, and thinking are clear. Whether or not they have great knowledge is another matter, for not all who are used by God possess great knowledge.

If our nous is renewed, our understanding will be keen. We shall know the will of God, the mind of God, and the word of God.

Consecration and the Renewing of the Nous

We now come to the second passage in the Bible which tells us of the need of having our nous renewed.

> I beseech you therefore, brethren, by the mercies of God, to present your bodies a living sacrifice, holy, acceptable to God, which is your spiritual service. And be not fashioned accord-

ing to this world: but be ye transformed by the renewing of
your mind, that ye may prove what is the good and acceptable and perfect will of God. (Rom. 12.1-2)

The word "mind" here is *nous* in the original. Once again it is
the renewing of the nous. Paul beseeches believers to present their
bodies to God in order to serve Him. The renewing of the nous is
based on consecration.

Friends, is there anything which holds you down? If you are
able to consecrate it by laying it all on the altar, your renewed
nous will be doubly strengthened by God for you to know His
heart and will as well as to think and understand the things of
God. You must make this transaction specifically. Then you will
be able to prove what is the acceptable will of God.

Many announce generally that they are willing to obey God in
all things, yet the fact remains they know not what they are saying
because they are far from such perfect obedience. At the time
when the Lord was soon to die, Peter boldly announced: "Even if I
must die with thee, yet will I not deny thee" (Matt. 26.35). Many
are like Peter. We do not know what God requires of us, hence we
will not grow spiritually. To determine the degree of spiritual
progress of a believer one need only inquire what God presently
requires of him. For instance, to a sinner newly saved God's requirement of him may be to forsake smoking, gambling, and other
external matters. We know that this is but the first step in spiritual
life; for there is not much depth to this. Gradually the new believer will be shown in addition that jealousy, pride, and things of
this nature are likewise bad; he is therefore making further progress. Still later, he is instructed by God that he must lay down his
own opinion in God's work; this indicates another step forward.

In a word, the requirement of God goes deeper all the time.
Some Christians know they should not smoke or gamble; others
know they ought not be proud or jealous; but these know nothing

else. We should offer to God according to what we know, and thus shall our nous be renewed. But at the same time, our renewed nous will tell us what we ought even further to offer to God.

After Renewal

The nous of too many Christians is like a kitchen window which is covered with oily dirt. After the nous is renewed, though, it becomes like a clean window which clearly lets in the sunlight. The believer is able to comprehend more and more what God requires of him. His nous has become most keen and alert. He can plainly know what God's requirement is. The reason many Christians do not know the will of God is because they do not have the proper receiving set. They can only guess and surmise what God's will is. But if their nous is renewed they will be able to know clearer and clearer the will of God.

(1) For example, *as to judgment.* "One man esteemeth one day above another: another esteemeth every day alike. Let each man be fully assured in his own mind" (Rom. 14.5). The "mind" here is *nous.* How do you judge right and wrong? Each judges according to his own nous.

(2) *As to understanding.* "Then opened he their mind, that they might understand the scriptures" (Luke 24.45). The "mind" here is again *nous.* Why did the Lord Jesus open their nous? That they might understand the Scriptures. Remember that we understand the Bible only after the Lord Jesus has opened our nous. As the nous is opened, the Scriptures are understood. Hence every time you read the Bible you should pray to God: "I humble myself as a child before You. I do not know nor do I understand the meaning of this passage. Please give me light."

It is not necessary for God to enable you to understand or possess the truth at the time of your reading the Word. Sometimes when you are walking on the street, or working at some job, or getting ready for bed, or getting up from bed, God opens your nous and makes you understand the truth. Once He opens your nous, you get to know fuller and fuller.

According to my own experience as well as the experience of many, God never reveals a truth in its entirety all at once. What we at first get from the reading of the Scriptures is fragmentary, but gradually we come to know the whole truth of God. Take as an illustration the truth of authority. I know a man in the Lord who for four to five months was held to this one truth. God showed him increasingly the truth concerning authority as given in the Bible.

(3) *As to preaching.* Once I was asked if one should prepare for the preaching. My answer was that he should prepare every day. We must receive from God daily. When we are shown in our nous the truth which God gives to us in our spirit, we shall come to know, within a short or a long period, the whole truth. A person does not prepare for preaching in two hours. This will be useless. Many spiritual people are able to receive yearly from God great and systematic truth in all clearness. God shows these truths to their nous that they may nourish both themselves and other people.

The Content of the Mind

Finally, concerning progress in this matter of the renewing of the mind, there is a part for you to do as well as a part for God to do. Let us remember that each and every renewed mind must be put under self-control. One must learn to start and to stop thinking. He should be able to control himself in a most natural fashion.

Do not let outside thought rule over you; if so, your thought is sick. This is not meant to mean, of course, that you should analyze your thoughts; for if you do you will suffer intense headache. Control of thought should be done naturally—just as closing and opening one's eyelids requires no thinking nor command but is done quite naturally. At first there will need to be some effort, but later on it can be done very naturally. We must control our thoughts, yet it should be accomplished naturally. Let us not analyze our thought lest we fall into pain and danger. This is something to be noticed.

OTHER TITLES YOU WILL WANT TO HAVE

By Watchman Nee

A Living Sacrifice
128 pages   1972   Paper

The Latent Power of the Soul
96 pages   1972   Paper

Spiritual Authority
192 pages   1972   Paper & Cloth

The Ministry of God's Word
282 pages   1971   Paper & Cloth

Spiritual Reality or Obsession
64 pages   1970   Paper

The Spiritual Man
3 Vols   1968   Paper & Cloth

The Release of the Spirit
96 pages   1965   Paper

By Stephen Kaung

The Songs of Degrees
Meditations on Fifteen Psalms
235 pages   1970   Paper & Cloth

ORDER FROM:

Christian Fellowship Publishers, Inc.
Box 58
Hollis, New York 11423